EGYPTIAN NUBIANS

To my Nubian friends and informants
for an invaluable learning experience
and humane companionship

EGYPTIAN NUBIANS

RESETTLEMENT AND YEARS OF COPING

Hussein M. Fahim

University of Utah Press
Salt Lake City

Library of Congress Cataloging in Publication Data
Fahim, Hussein M., 1934-
  Egyptian Nubians.

  Includes bibliographical references and index.
  1. Nubians—Egypt. 2. Land Settlement—Egypt.
3. Social change—Case studies. 4. Aswan High
Dam (Egypt) I. Title.
DT133.N79F33 1983   305.8'931   82–24723
ISBN 0–87480–215–6

Contents

v

ILLUSTRATIONS

Preface

In a recent publication entitled *Uprooting and Development*, editors George Coelho and Paul Ahmed indicated that "throughout the long history of human development people around the world have been relocated in order to survive" (1980:6). In the present-day world, however, the uprooting of communities or entire populations has been happening with unprecedented speed and abruptness in both the environmental and social arenas. "These changes are accelerated and amplified by the diffusion of technology to the point that the impact of change is massive in scale and global in scope" (Coelho and Ahmed 1980:7). There is reason to assume that as countries, whether developed or undeveloped, increase their capabilities for energy development and more efficient use of natural resources, more and more groups will be displaced, either on their initiative or against their will. "It is also reasonable to expect these groups to experience complex problems in adjusting to new surroundings" (Trimble 1980:473).

Whatever the reasons for and the extent of community displacement may be, uprooting or resettling people is a dramatic human event that creates stress, produces stress reaction, and requires the use of strategies to cope with a wide range of pressures. While all changes require use of coping strategies, forced migration or resettlement constitutes an abrupt form of social change. It is disruptive, occasionally tragic, and in many cases generates irreversible problems. The most recent and perhaps most striking cases of uprooting and resettlement of entire communities involving large numbers of people are those associated with the construction of hydroelectric projects for water and land development purposes. A case in point is the displacement of

vii

approximately one hundred thousand Nubians in Egypt and the Sudan in connection with the construction of the Aswan High Dam.

Since 1960, when plans to build the Aswan High Dam were announced, local and foreign anthropologists have conducted a number of studies among the Nubians of Egypt and the Sudan who would be displaced by the project. Over a period of two decades or so, the Nubians have witnessed two stages of this anthropological research. The first stage consisted of a wide range of archaeological excavations and conservation projects as well as ethnological surveys that compiled a comprehensive record of traditional Nubian culture. The "Ethnological Survey of Egyptian Nubia," a 1960–64 study by the Social Research Center of the American University in Cairo, was a major product of this research. In the Sudan, probably the major systematic anthropological study among the affected Sudanese Nubians was conducted 1962–64 by the Kronenbergs, a German anthropologist and his wife (1963, 1964, 1965a, 1965b).

In 1964, during the relocation process, some preliminary reports on the pre-resettlement studies of Egyptian Nubia were presented and discussed at an international symposium in Aswan (Fernea 1966). While these papers presented interesting and valuable information on the Nubian culture, it was too late to use this knowledge in relocation planning.

The second stage of research, which occurred after the resettlement in 1964, described, analyzed, and assessed the impact of displacement on the traditional Nubian life-style. Unlike the earlier studies, this second stage of anthropological research among the displaced Nubians was by and large redundant, sporadic, and less systematic. Too many interested parties were involved in the research—government departments, research institutions, local and foreign researchers, and students —and there was no coordination of research. As a result, the Nubians grew tired of all these studies and in some cases resented providing information. Some Nubians were even antagonistic toward researchers, expressing their feeling that research had not helped them in solving their resettlement problems (Fahim 1977).

During the past decade, several publications have appeared on the effects of relocation on Nubia and its people. These publications concerned a wide range of anthropological fields and topics: archaeology, physical anthropology, linguistics, folklore, and cultural anthropology (e.g., Fernea and Gerster 1973; Adams 1977; Hohenwart 1979; Kennedy 1978). In addition to this host of recent publications, a Nubian exhibit was displayed at the Brooklyn Museum in New York from September to December 1978, from whence it moved to the Seattle Museum of Art for a three-month period in 1979, and later travelled to the Haags Gemeentemuseum in The Hague, Netherlands. Entitled "Africa in Antiquity: The Arts of Ancient Nubia and the Sudan," it was the first international exhibition devoted to the arts of ancient Nubia. Over 250 objects had been loaned by twenty-five institutions and collectors. These objects belong to different Nubian cultures that span a period of over five millennia; they were catalogued in two volumes.

The Staatliche Museum in West Berlin and the Brooklyn Museum of New York co-organized the exhibition and also held an international symposium in New York from September 28 to October 1, 1978. The proceedings of the symposium were scheduled to appear in a special issue of *Meroitica*, Humboldt University, East Berlin. Later, in April 1980 for the annual meeting of the American Research Center in Egypt, held in San Francisco, Aleya Roshdi of Wayne State University organized a session on "Nubia Before and After Resettlement." Undoubtedly, these two events, i.e., the Brooklyn exhibit and the San Francisco meeting, indicate a continuing interest in Nubian culture, past and present. They also made Nubia internationally known in the academic arena; and the Nubian case seems to have become one of the better documented, modern ethnographic studies.

In this book I largely draw upon my previous publications, presenting a synthesis of my Nubian research findings among the Egyptian Nubians. I should indicate, however, that I had the opportunity to visit with the resettled Sudanese Nubians on several occasions. I paid three visits to the Sudanese Nubians on their new site. My first two visits were made in 1969 and in 1973, respectively, for the purpose of investigating the early stages of physical displacement and means of coping in an unfamiliar habitat under new social and economic conditions. The third visit took place in March 1980, nearly sixteen years after the resettlement. Thayer Scudder and I worked together to identify the stages that the scheme of land settlement and development at Khashm el-Girba had gone through and the factors which had contributed to both failures and successes.

Although I did not initially design my Nubian study to become longitudinal, it just happened that I followed up the resettlement case from time to time over a period of nearly seventeen years, from 1963 through 1980. While the time perspective is very important in reporting on long-term studies, the book is not structured to provide separate reports on each period of fieldwork among the Nubians. Instead, it focuses on certain problems of resettlement and discusses specific issues that have happened since relocation. The major thrust of this work relates to the question of how people, culture, and environment interact and influence one another throughout the process of adjusting to displacement and promoting socioeconomic change. In addition, it aims to provide a conceptual and policy-oriented treatment of resettlement schemes.

This book is also written as an anthropological account concerning the human experience of the displaced Egyptian Nubians. (For information on the Sudanese resettlement see Fahim 1973, 1979b, 1980; Dafalla 1975; Sorbo 1977a, 1977b, 1980; Agouba 1980; Hale 1979.) If I were to conduct the Nubian study anew, it would not be at all the way I have presented it here, for the researcher has learned much from this experience and would therefore plan his research work differently.

The book includes four parts, in eleven chapters. The parts and chapters address selected issues and do not include all possible resettlement problems, concepts, and policies. Although some topics or chapters are short on specific data or may raise questions that still require answers, it is important to have the information at this point to reflect upon and learn from for future research and planning. The main objective in presenting the Nubian resettlement case is to arouse the interest and concern of readers, especially those engaged in resettlement, be they settlers, administrators, or researchers, in order that they might better understand the complexity of the situation and become more aware of the instinctive need for mankind to preserve individual cultures.

Throughout the stages of collection, analysis, and writing of the Nubian data, I have received both financial and academic support from several institutions. In this regard, I wish to acknowledge the invaluable assistance rendered over almost a decade from 1963 to 1973 by the Social Research Center of the American University in Cairo. To both the former and present directors of the Center, Professors

Laila El Hamamsy and Saad Gaddalla, respectively, who provided me with the necessary means to pursue research among the displaced Nubians: my thanks.

I also wish to acknowledge and express appreciation for the excellent work undertaken by the Center's research and secretarial staff, who assisted me in the office and during fieldwork. I am particularly grateful for the assistance rendered by Kamal El Zayat, Zeinab Gamal, Omar Abdel Hamid, Atef Hanna, Esmat Kheir, Fikri Abdel Wahab, Hekmat Wassef, and Awatef Youniss. Two of the research assistants, Zeinab Gamal and Fikri Abdel Wahab, were Nubians, and I was especially intrigued by their insights and contribution to the understanding of the Nubian culture.

In 1977–78, the Wenner-Gren Foundation for Anthropological Research was kind enough to give me a grant-in-aid (No. 3108) toward the writing of the Nubian material for publication. The candid discussions and insightful dialogues that have been occurring since 1975 with Mrs. Lita Osmundsen, the Foundation's director of research, are acknowledged here for their constructive and intellectual substance.

While in residence (1975–78) at the Center for International Studies of the University of Pittsburgh, I also received full support from the late Dr. Karl Beck, then director of the Center, and the secretarial staff, especially Henrietta Moss, in analyzing the Nubian material and writing a preliminary draft of this book.

Several of my peers and senior colleagues have read parts or all of the preliminary draft; thanks to all of them for their invaluable comments, particularly to Dr. Robert Fernea and Mrs. Elizabeth Fernea of the University of Texas, Austin, and to Drs. Elizabeth Colson and Eugene Hammel of the University of California, Berkeley.

I also appreciate the invaluable comments made by Dr. Michael Cernea, the senior sociologist at the World Bank, and would like to mention here with gratitude the approval by Mr. Alfonso Pesada, senior power engineer at the Energy Division of the World Bank, to include some of my observations and notes obtained while on appraisal missions in connection with the Kpong resettlement project in Ghana.

My long-term academic association with Dr. Thayer Scudder of the California Institute of Technology has been exceptionally and intellectually rewarding. Over a period of more than a decade he has shown a scholarly concern in following up my Nubian research, carefully reading my material, then constructively and enthusiastically advising me. I also worked closely with several other people while in the process of data collection and analysis; and in this regard I wish to refer to my research work in London with Katherine Helmer, a senior researcher at the Institute of Man and Science, and Drs. William Vogt and Marvin Mickle, professors of Engineering and System Analysis at the University of Pittsburgh, with whom I was involved in a preliminary attempt to develop a mathematical model of relocation variables and processes (see Fahim, Vogt, and Mickle 1979).

Furthermore, my thanks are extended to include those who reviewed the book's manuscript for the University of Utah Press; their points were well taken, and their comments have been extremely helpful in preparing the final draft of this book.

At the University of Utah, where I am currently a research professor with the Middle East Center and the Department of Anthropology, I have found substantial support for my research and writing projects. I am thankful to both Drs. Khosrow Mostofi, the Center's director, and John McCullough, the Department's chairman. I wish to acknowledge the intellectual insights that Dr. Irwin Altman and Ms. Mary Gauvain, both of the Department of Psychology, have contributed to my analysis of the housing component of the resettlement scheme. I wish also to acknowledge and express my appreciation for the editing by Norma Mikkelsen at the University of Utah Press, the work on the book by other staff members of the Press, and the typing services rendered by Ursula Hanly at the Department of Anthropology. Louise Weidner's assistance in proofreading and compiling the index was invaluable.

Several other people have directly or indirectly contributed to the undertaking of this Nubian study throughout all its stages; I am most obliged to them all, especially my wife, Ehsan Fahim, who has long been anxious to see the Nubian book in print and the research findings in use.

PART I

TECHNICAL DEVELOPMENT AND FORCED CHANGE

The title of Part I is borrowed from Elizabeth Colson's book, The Social Consequences of Resettlement, *in which she views mass technological development as hurtful and points out that "this fact has largely been ignored by all those who plan and implement it." She also argues that in "planning drastic alterations in environment that uproot populations or make old adjustment impossible, they count engineering cost but not the social costs. After all, they do not think of themselves as paying the latter. Some people no doubt like radical change. The majority probably likes variety only so long as it is an embroidery upon the reassuring familiarity of customary routines, well known paths and scenes, and the ease of accustomed relationships" (1971:1).*

This view does not necessarily imply an argument "against all change or against development. This would be folly," Colson explains, "for people have been making decisions that altered their lives and the structure of their communities since human history began" (1971:3). However, forced change should not be seen as or attributed only to technical development; natural disasters and political upheavals may cause similar if not more suffering. Nonetheless, Colson advises that "it is folly to allow technology to determine policy."

Chapter One presents glimpses into the past of a land and a people, both of which had suffered as a result of "technological development." Two dams erected across the Nile have gradually wiped out the land, forcing the Nubians to leave and establish a new life in an unfamiliar habitat. Data in the first chapter have been compiled from a wide range of literature based on first-hand information. I also visited Nubia two times, in February 1963 and in March 1964; each

3

visit lasted two weeks. My objective here is to describe certain basic characteristics of Nubia, its people, and elements of their social organization. Detailed studies of different aspects of traditional Nubian culture, i.e., those observed and recorded prior to relocation, are now available in a number of publications in English, e.g., Fernea and Gerster (1973), Adams (1975), Keating (1978), and Kennedy (1978).

Chapter Two examines the "Nubian Exodus," to use Dafalla's book title (1975), in the context of building dams and creating lakes over Nubia. It also discusses aspects of a different perception of these engineering projects constructed across the Nile. While the sponsor, i.e., the Egyptian government, conceived these dams, and especially the recently built High Dam, in the context of a "positive technical development," the affected people, the Nubians in this case, found the actions destructive to their history and culture. Although the government was quite aware of the adverse effect the dam would have on the inhabitants of the Nubian Valley, that effect was conceived as a minor cost compared to the assumed nationwide benefits of the dam; and the government felt responsible for providing a new site and better living conditions for the displaced Nubians, assuring them of an efficient move into the new area and fair compensation for the material loss of their homes and belongings.

The government's concern was also reflected in the frequent visits of Egypt's president, the vice-president, and other top officials to Nubia and their expressed willingness to take Nubian customs and demands into consideration when planning and implementing the relocation scheme. While Chapter Two deals with the conceptualization of resettlement and the policies of community building, Chapter Three addresses the challenging task of implementation. It describes the physical move of the Nubians out of their homeland and portrays how things were in the new land at the time of arrival. I credit the title of this chapter, "Leaving Nubia on Noah's Ark," to a Nubian who told me that he had recalled Noah's story while sailing down the Nile to the "unknown."

One major conclusion of Chapter Three is that resettlement planning and implementation are not unidemensional, neither can they be viewed as one-shot activities. Rather, it is a multifaceted process that, if properly conceived and executed, should include monitoring and consideration for the timing, sequence, and diversity and interrelated-

ness of variables that constitute the structure of the resettlement schemes and determine its function as well.

Also, as Chapter Three and the subsequent Part II demonstrate, good intentions are not enough to ease the suffering of people, and big promises cannot help toward making a decent living; resettlement is not only a complex technical endeavor, but also a serious human issue and a challenging task. In several parts of the book readers will identify areas of success and failure and recognize the reasons. Yet, the main pitfall lies, in my view, in looking at people as "miscellaneous items" on the agenda of technical development projects.

Chapter One
Nubia and Glimpses into Its Past

Nothing in the world can equal the sweetness of the mornings and evenings in Nubia. The very act of breathing is a luxury, as though the lungs were enjoying a holiday. I could see to read by moonlight, when the moon was only in the first quarter. The air was calm, the leaves of the tree motionless, no need to call "silence" for all nature seemed in a trance. To say it is charming would express but little. It is literally enchanting; it is inexpressible.

> Nubia as described by a nineteenth-century traveller (Greener 1962:43). When I first visited Nubia in 1963, nearly one century later, I found it almost the same (HMF).

THE SETTING

The Nile, Egypt's heart and nerve center, takes the shape of a lotus flower (Figure 1) as it flows across the northeastern African desert and through the remote lower part of the country where Nubia once existed. Much of Nubia now lies under water and will remain so forever. This part of the Nile Valley covers areas in both Egypt and the Sudan. The region known as Nubia is the boundaryless area stretching from the Nile's First Cataract, in the north, to the southern end of its great bend, midway between the Third and Fourth Cataracts (Figure 2). Rolf Herzog, a German historian, defined Nubia as "that part of the Nile valley where the inhabitants speak Nubian" (Gerster 1963:606).

THE PEOPLE

Although the people of Nubia usually identify themselves as Nubians, there are basic linguistic and ethnic differences. In Nubia there

7

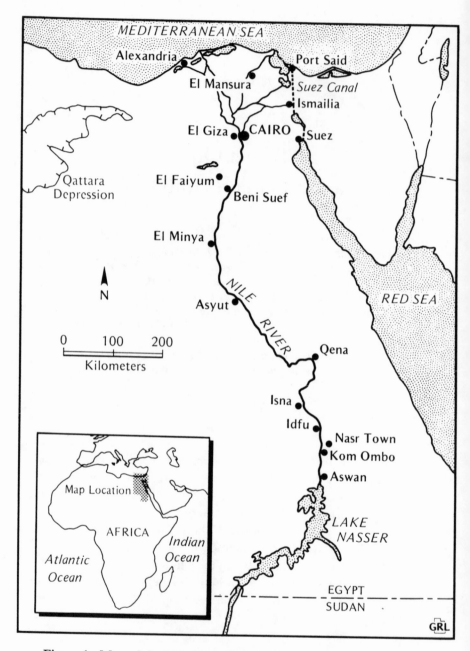

Figure 1. Map of the Nile River showing Lake Nasser.

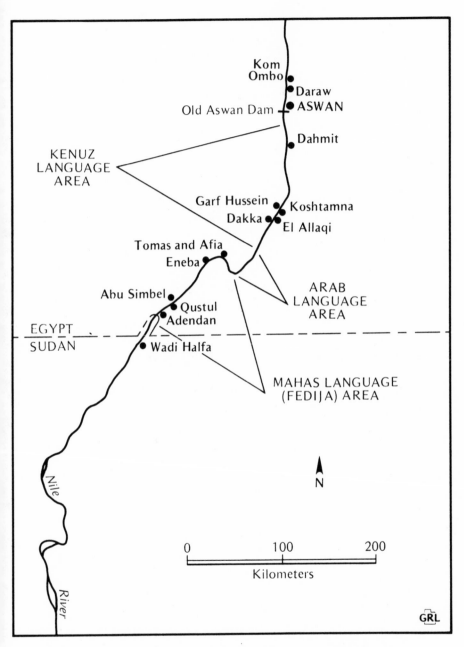

Figure 2. Map of Old Nubia showing locations of the Nubian groups.

were three linguistic groups, each inhabiting a separate part of the region: the Kenuz group, who occupied the territory from Aswan south along the Nile for a distance of nearly 150 kilometers and speak a dialect called Metouki; the Arabs, who previously settled in communities along the next 40 kilometers to the south and speak Arabic (this group claims Bedouin traditions and has cultural affiliations with the Arabic-speaking tribes in the Sudan); and the Fedija, who lived along 130 kilometers of the Nile in the southern extremity of Egyptian Nubia and speak Mahas. "In spite of the isolation in which the Nubians had been living for ages, the influence of the Arab culture and language became stronger and stronger. The sedentary Nubians [retained] their dialects and especially the women did not know Arabic before they were moved to the new settlements [in] Egypt. Men, however, who had taken jobs in Arab-speaking countries were bi-lingual for two or sometimes even three generations. In school only Arabic was taught which—of course—was an advantage for the children and the youth when they were displaced" (Hohenwart 1975:186).

Nubians constitute an ethnic group of nearly 120,000 people (0.29 percent of the total population of Egypt at the time of relocation in 1963), including those who work or live in cities. Skin color and language serve to differentiate Nubians from other ethnic groups in Egypt. Because of their primarily Negroid rather than Caucasoid ancestry, Nubians are darker skinned than the average Egyptian. The most common skin color ranges from light to medium brown. Nubians have mediterranean-type facial features, and their hair is frizzy or kinky.

"Back in history, especially since the period of Fatimid rule . . . , Nubia was referred to as the 'land of blacks' for its involvement in an extensive slave trade" (Kennedy 1977:17). While the Arabic term "Barberi" was common and is still used by some Egyptians when referring to Nubians, it was used, in my view, in a linguistic context— the way the ancient Greeks used the term "Ber Ber" to refer to neighboring groups who spoke incomprehensible (to them) languages.

In comparing the Nubians to black Americans, Fernea and Gerster comment: "The persistence of exclusively Nubian villages, repositories of a distinct culture, has helped this people at all times to retain a sense of who they are. The black American is now attempting to discover a heritage all but obscured by generations of white domination" (1973:4). Because of their dislike of manual labor and their reputation for being exceptionally clean and honest, Nubian men and boys were always favored for domestic work as doorkeepers, waiters, custodians, cooks, etc. These jobs, which required no skills, very often were passed from father to son, and in case of openings Nubians recruited each other on the basis of kinship ties or ethnic affiliation. Thus, it became traditional for Egyptian society to think of Nubians for these types of jobs; it was not merely a case of discrimination against them. Because of their good character, Nubians were generally well regarded by other Egyptians. Nevertheless, because of the low status associated with their kind of work, they were also perceived as having lower social attributes and individual abilities.

The Sudanese Nubians, known as the Halfans, originally resided in Wadi Halfa District, a region extending for about 170 kilometers along the Nile between the Egyptian border in the north and the Dal Cataract, Sudan, in the south. The Halfans have their own language, known as Sukkot, and Arabic is used as a second language, mainly for communication with non-Halfan groups. The Halfans previously inhabited a very narrow valley with desert on both sides that sometimes extended to the edge of the river. The climate was dry with no rainfall, but the Nile, date trees, gracious mud houses, and sand were all physical elements that were unique and desirable to the Halfans. In addition, ancient civilizations had made this area one the most important communities in the Sudan. The visitor to this area "was often overwhelmed by its archaeological wealth in ancient temples, forts, vaults, churches and mosques" (Scaff 1961/62).

While the Nubians constituted the dominant group living in the Nubian Valley, there were nomadic groups who resided in this desert-like wilderness that flanked the valley. Their exact number is not known, but it is estimated to have been only a few thousand. Perhaps the most frequent nomadic visitors, and sometimes settlers, in Nubia were the pastoral tribes of the Red Sea hills, whose higher elevations near the coast have long supported a nomadic population. However, the barren desert between the valley and hills discouraged the development of a close symbiotic interaction and prevented the perennial conflicts between the desert tribes and the villages that had been characteristic of other parts of the Middle East (Adams 1977:56).

These nomadic tribes were totally overlooked in the resettlement scheme on the basis that they constituted an extremely small portion of the inhabitants below the scheduled dam. For the majority of these nomads the formation of the lake depleted their natural resources, and they, consequently, reacted by retreating deep into the Eastern Desert. Some moved to Daraw, a market town located some thirty-five kilometers north of the city of Aswan. These nomads are likely to return to the shoreline of the lake if any significant vegetation develops in the area.

INDIGENOUS ECONOMY

Nubia was a poor country in the economic sense and in terms of resources. Nubia lived basically on what this portion of the Nile, namely the Nubian Valley, could provide. The rise and fall of the water level regulated the annual cycle of subsistence economy. According to Hohenwart, "In Nubia the water covered the strips of land along the river from ancient times to the turn of this century from June to September so that crops could be grown from October to May. The moist ground used to be fertile enough to guarantee [a] good harvest" (1975:183). As a result of limited arable lands and dependency on the water level in this part of the Nile Valley, labor migration became a means of coping with the finite economic resources in Nubia.

Agriculture was then the basis of the indigenous economy. There were approximately 15,000 feddans under cultivation, with 11,600 watered by government irrigation pumping stations. (One feddan equals 1.038 acres.) The people subsisted on meager gains from agriculture and on remittances that varied between one and five Egyptian pounds per month per family. (One Egyptian pound equaled $2.40 U.S. in the early sixties.) In 1962, one year before resettlement, a government survey showed that as much as 73 percent of the Arab Nubians and 70 percent of the Fedija population claimed to be receiving cash remittances, but as few as 57 percent among the Kenuz.

The main crops were millet and dates. The latter were a basic item of the Nubian diet as well as an essential symbolic element of almost all ceremonies. Vegetables were cultivated on a very small scale and fruits were scarce. Domesticated animals such as goats, sheep, and small herds of cattle replaced dates as a major local source of cash income in many parts of Nubia since less time and effort were needed to grow fodder than the previously mentioned crops. Domesticated animals were also important as a source of meat, milk, and hides. Nubian women showed great concern for their animals by devoting much of their daily activities to animal care.

Labor migration had several effects on the structure and function of Nubian society and particularly on its demographic composition. It resulted in a population that was made up mostly of women, old men, and children. Three years before relocation, the 1960 census showed Nubia with a population of 17,785 males and 30,243 females; this was in addition to approximately seventy thousand Nubians living then in cities, as estimated by Geiser (1966:167). The sex ratio in Nubia varied from one area to another. The magnitude of the emigration phenomenon throughout Nubian modern history is reflected by the long-standing low ratio of men to women (78:100 as compared to 101:100 for the entire country in the 1960 census). In some of the Nubian villages the ratio was as low as 37:100, while other villages had no young men at all. In addition, the fifteen-to-forty age group was very small, and the number of aged people relatively high. As Geiser has pointed out, "the high number of disabled aged men, widows, or women may suggest that the Nubian village was a kind of refuge for both men and women who, in regard to city life, had become of marginal value in social and economic terms" (1966:168).

The migration of able-bodied men resulted in a high proportion of working women in Nubia. For the years before relocation, the 1960 census showed the working population composed of about twelve thousand persons, of whom almost one-third were women. While women made up 5 percent of the total working population in Egypt, the number of working Nubian women was as high as 14 percent of the total working population in Nubia according to the 1964 report on Nubia by the National Research Center. In cases where women could not farm, the land was usually left under the care of a relative of a friend. Migrants used to contribute toward buying seed and fertilizer in return for a share of the crop.

Sharecropping developed as a result of labor migration and constituted a basic element in the agrarian structure of the Nubian community. However, the Nubian pattern of sharecropping was unique. In the Egyptian delta, the practice grew out of a feudalistic situation in which foreigners acquired control of large areas of land and the peasants were obliged to till the land for a relatively small share of the crop. But in Nubia, as Fernea pointed out, the landowner and the sharecropper were frequently relatives. The supervisor was seldom richer than the person who tilled the land. In other words, there was little if any class distinction and formal relationship associated with sharecropping, unlike the situation among the rest of the Egyptian peasantry (Fernea 1962).

The general lack of motivation to farm did not mean that Nubians lost interest in land ownership; they were interested in owning land as an investment and as an access to status. But agricultural work has never appealed to them. (They differ in this respect from other Egyptian peasants, who often consider farming the most meritorious and blessed of all occupations.) City life appealed to Nubians so much that some families sent their boys to the cities regardless of economic difficulties because they considered it the proper training for better future work.

ELEMENTS OF SOCIAL ORGANIZATION

The hamlet and the village were two basic elements in the social organization of Nubian communities. However, there were variations among the three Nubian groups regarding the significance attached to either kinship affiliation or territorial residence. Lineage appeared to be more important in the north than in the south. It organized many of the political, economic, religious, and marital affairs of the Kenuz community. In the south, the village was more important for determining social identity than the lineage. Most village activities were carried out on the basis of reciprocity, which was developed in terms of friendship and neighborhood ties rather than kinship relations. Many corporate functions that were handled by the tribe among the Kenuz were village functions among the Mahas-speaking groups.

Nevertheless, the patrilineage still had its function in the south as a security organization, although its support was rarely invoked. In the Arab area, agnatic descent was a basic element of community social organization. The Nubians of the area tended to have inclusive lineages that extended outside Nubia. However, as Fernea (1962) indicates, such units were of little additional significance although they were a focus of strong loyalties based on village or district residence.

The lowest level of social organization was the hamlet (*naja*), which consisted of a number of households and was the smallest named segment of a village. Physically, the hamlets and hence the villages were situated along the banks of the Nile, one beside the other. The dividing lines between the groups of hamlets (about 530) were often marked by bends in the river, which separated one village from the next.

Socially, each hamlet was a distinct unit in terms of the obligations of mutual aid which bound its members. The obligations were ordinarily activated in times of need. Members of the same hamlet would work together in the fields, for example. Also, whenever a woman in the hamlet went into labor, her women neighbors rushed to help her, and the men gathered to comfort and support her husband. In addition, the hamlet was the locus of the customary mutual visiting that often took place during the month of Ramadan, during which Moslems fast from dawn to sunset.

Yet the village also had a marked role of cohesiveness; it served as a ritual unit which carried out as a whole all rites that were performed for marriages, deaths, and other occasions. The village also maintained a cemetery, a mosque, and a school and, in addition, was an administrative unit where the mayor had a guest house.

Above this level of inclusiveness, two units existed: the districts and Nubia as a whole. The district was the unit where local administrative business was conducted. Nubia was divided into thirty-nine districts, each known as a *nahia* (sometimes referred to as an *omedia*) and composed of a number of *najas*. For each district there was a government-appointed *omda* (a headman who served as the liaison between the people and the government). To maintain security he was furnished with one armed guard for each *naja*. These administrative districts were not socially organized and their boundaries were arbitrarily determined. Nevertheless, a district's boundaries seemed to represent the limits for social activities important to Nubians. Nubians outside Nubia used to identify themselves first as Nubians and then as coming from a particular *nahia* or *omedia*, which was an important clue to their social identity (Horton 1964:9).

Beyond the social structure and function of both the hamlet and village and that of the administrative role of the districts, Nubia was conceived as the "homeland" for all Nubians, who believed to be united by the "fact" of common agnatic descent. This theme of a common descent was even extended to those Nubians living in the Sudan. Nubians always felt that the Egyptian–Sudanese border was no more than an arbitrary political line that had no cultural meaning. Prior to resettlement, Nubia was administratively semi-independent. The limited population size, scarce resources, physical isolation, and remoteness from the administrative centers in Cairo discouraged a wide range of government activities in Nubia. Nonetheless, there were quite a few activities sponsored and controlled by the government, such as communication, education, and circulation of goods.

Some Nubian villages had never seen government officials because they rarely left their headquarters in Eneba, a frontier village (Figure 2), and because an absence of roads meant travel was only by boat or donkey. The post boat, making two trips every week and stopping at major villages, linked distant villages with one another and Nubia in general with the city of Aswan, and, thus, with the remainder of the country.

Egyptian Nubia's lack of contact with the central administration and the rest of the country helped Nubians maintain their own spoken dialects as well as the customs and traditions of the group. However, they shared with non-Nubian groups a common religious affiliation, Islam, and related cultural values. Most Nubians speak Arabic, Egypt's common language. The informal and modest style of life Nubians had enjoyed in their old setting as well as their semi-independence from the central administration developed distinct personality characteristics, such as dignity, hospitality, and tolerance. Above all, they are a peaceful people, as Fernea and Gerster described them in the title of their book (1973).

Status differences existed, but they did not apply so much to groups as they did to individuals. Drawing upon a novel by a Nubian writer, Young indicates that "a person's rank in his community is determined by a number of distinct factors, the two most important of which are cash incomes and land ownership. Those who are ridden by debt are looked down upon. Landlessness, also, is regarded as a great misfortune because it often forces a man to rely on the charity of his neighbors. Reduction to economic dependency is painfully humiliating and is to be avoided at all costs. Furthermore, large landowners have significant influence on local government representatives and enjoy the respect of the villagers; they are referred to with the honorific . . . master of a portion of land" (Young 1978).

Nonetheless, as Hohenwart pointed out, "A stratification of every village community was perceptible though the Nubians themselves denied its existence. They disliked the idea of class-differences. Because of their brotherly love, they stressed the quality of status. Nevertheless, there [was] a village council which [consisted of] the representatives of the leading tribes, chaired by the *Omda*, the Mayor. If any difficulties arose within the village community, they tried to settle them among themselves and avoid [taking] any case outside their territory. Besides the village-councillors there were the merchants and the teachers who represented the intellectual leaders, then there was the village folk with a slight admixture of negroes, the descendants of former slaves. Social rank and financial standard should never be stressed among the Nubian society" (1975:188).

FAMILY AND RESIDENCE PATTERN

The 1960 census taken three years prior to relocation reported the existence of 16,066 families living in Nubia. The Nubian extended family was patrilineal, patrilocal, and mostly monogamous. The preferred marriage was within the kin group with special value placed on cross-cousin marriage. Intermarriage between different Nubian groups was rare. Nevertheless, many Nubian migrants living in cities were not bound by this rule and married non-Nubian women. Divorce was frowned upon by both tradition and religion; it was regarded as disastrous for women due to the lack of remarriage opportunities in a society where women outnumbered men.

Residence based on kinship bonds not only determined the nature of interpersonal relationships among the inhabitants of each *naja*, but also encouraged the development of patterns of economic and social duties. The residence pattern, for instance, encouraged the system of purchase on credit among the members of the *naja*. It was customary for Nubians to use one room in the house as a variety store, and people took their commodities on credit until remittances were received or crops sold.

The structure of the Nubian family also promoted certain social and economic patterns among the members of a household. For example, it was observed that "nuclear families residing together are viewed by the Nubians as a unit and they stressed particularly the cooperation and inter-dependence of its members inside the home. But outside of the home, each of the married women living together is expected to fulfill her social duties and obligations independently as in the case of the Aza or mourning ceremony, the wedding and the karama celebration organized by a family to fulfill a vow. . . . Males are expected to share in the household expenses, and if a father and son work together in the field, both share the crop obtained. Husbands are responsible for supporting their wives as soon as they leave their own father's home and come to join the husband's family" (B. Heikal 1966:2).

In the case of polygamous marriages, B. Heikal found that in the Nubian *naja* of Ismailia, each wife had her own house (1966:3). She found also that co-wives resisted being considered as one unit. As long as co-wives were socially and economically distinct, cordial social relations would exist among them. On many occasions, they visited each other's houses, and relationships between their children were friendly if they came as visitors. Widows and widowers, who constituted 35.5 percent of the Nubian population in 1960, as well as elderly couples used to receive daily care and help from their kin living next to them.

As different observers of Nubian culture recorded, the inhabitants of each *naja* were members of some extended families who shared a common ancestor. It was customary for members of a family to build their houses adjacent to each other in order to have help nearby in case of need. One observer of a Kenuz village noted that hospitality for a guest was not restricted to one household. The construction of a new house or nuptial room was an occasion for neighbors to manifest their affinity and solidarity. Men and women worked together according to their abilities and skills; the owner of the house provided food, tea, and cigarettes for the workers (Abdel Wahab 1964).

Close interpersonal relationships, such as those illustrated above, existed only among the members of small units such as the family and the *naja*. Beyond these in-group relationships, developed through the residence pattern, Nubians tended to be cautious and reserved. In-group feeling and the pride that was associated with it was evident in the nicknames of the *najas*, which were believed to express distinctive *naja* personalities. Although they readily identified themselves as

Nubians when with members of other Egyptian groups, Nubians tended to specify their area of origin and sometimes the *naja*. Competition and conflict existed among the groups and *najas* and were manifested in different forms. Several *najas*, for instance, took pride in having the shrines of famous *shaykhs* (ancestral saints). In the Kenuz community, tribes competed with each other over the celebration of the *moulid* (an annual commemoration of a saint's birthday). Within the boundaries of the *naja*, Nubian families competed with each other in celebrating the ceremonies of circumcision, wedding, and birth. They sometimes competed in the kind of *nadr* (vow) they had for some shrines.

In the case of disputes, the rule was to avoid the intervention of people other than close relatives and friends. The Nubian community was self-regulating, capable of solving its own problems internally by peaceful means. Statistics revealed a low crime and theft rate compared to groups in other parts of the country. Nubians attributed that to two distinctive traits of Nubian personality: honesty and a belief in peaceful coexistence. While this may be the case, the mechanism of social control should not be overlooked. When dishonest acts occurred, the people involved were able to put matters right in their own way rather than reporting the incident to the police or taking the disagreement to court. Nubian communities preferred to limit outside knowledge of dishonesty and disputes to as few persons as possible. To take a case outside the community was considered an admission of failure for the whole community.

Fascinated by the community solidarity and prevailing spirit of togetherness and help, Hohenwart observed that "there was an unwritten law in existence that help had to be given to anyone [in absolute secrecy]. If a poor family had debts in a shop, the shop-keeper would never have stopped [serving] these people knowing that one day one of their relations would turn up in order to pay the bill. The Nubians were sensitive to tactlessness. Because of their noble attitude not even servants could be given money directly, but only by a mediator. Otherwise, one might have hurt their feelings. Intertribal aid did not need laws nor rules. Institutionalized welfare was quite unknown" (1975:188).

The Nubian House and Community Spirit

After the two heightenings of the first Aswan dam in 1912 and 1933, Nubians set up new villages on hills beyond the reach of the annual floods. They reconstructed their houses in the traditional architectural style. The houses that composed the *naja*s were strung out in single file along one bank or the other of the Nile. In an impressionistic description of Nubian houses, an eminent Egyptian architect wrote: "It was a new world for all of us, whole villages of houses spacious, lovely, clean, and harmonious. There was nothing like them in Egypt" (Fatehi 1966:2). Reflecting on the unique architectural feature of the Nubian villages, Georg Gerster, a Swiss traveller and photographer, said, "I believe that the architecture of the Nubia house aims to ease the mind of the departing husband. A rectangular wall encloses several one-story rooms which open on an inner court—a common ground plan in this part of the world, but in Nubia the walls are higher than elsewhere. I saw veritable castles, looking as if they had been designed jointly by a confectioner and a fortress engineer. ... I looked at one of those stately houses: the palace of the wife who stayed behind—and her prison" (1963:611). Other observers have found Nubian houses large and spacious. Built on one floor, with walls as high as six or sometimes eight meters, each house was composed of several wide rooms roofed by either brick vault-and-dome construction or palm trunks and reeds, which in both cases suited the hot, dry weather. These rooms, which had several holes near the roof for ventilation, usually opened onto a wide open-air courtyard, which was an essential part of any Nubian house. Most residents had outdoor sleeping places on clay platforms in the yard for the summertime. These wide courtyards were useful, since additional rooms could be added as finances permitted. (It was the custom for a bride to reside with her husband's family.)

Interestingly enough, as Fatehi (1966) points out, the *mahr* (brideprice) was often equivalent to the cost of the nuptial room. In the courtyard there were usually some big jars for the water that women and girls brought every day from the Nile. Other jars were used for food and seed storage. A kitchen with a clay oven was also essential. Baking bread, the most important item of Nubian diet, constituted an important part of women's daily activities. It was the custom to serve fresh hot bread to guests as a gesture of hospitality. Different kinds of bread were baked for different occasions. For example, *chadi* (wheat bread) was baked especially for the preparation of *fatta*, a symbolic meal of bread in lamb soup that is covered with rice and pieces of meat. The serving of this dish was an essential part of almost all Nubian religious and social ceremonies.

Particularly important to the Nubians was a space for entertaining visitors: the *mastaba* or low clay bench running along the front of the house and the *madiafa* or guest room were essential parts of the Nubian house. It was common to see a group of neighbors sitting together on the *mastaba* of any house. Tea with milk, a favorite Nubian beverage, was usually served to the group by the owner of the house. Male neighbors, who usually were members of one extended family, used to gather from time to time to have lunch or dinner together. Women sometimes did the same thing providing that each one brought her own dish. During Ramadan, I observed in a southern Nubian village the custom of one house offering dishes of *shihria* (vermicelli) to members of the neighboring houses. Around these dishes, men held a social gathering while they ate, talked, and smoked the *shisha* (water pipe), which they passed around. Observers in other Nubian villages have also noted that the Nubian house was the center of most social activities.

Nubians decorated walls and rooms, particularly the nuptial room, with baskets, plates with artistic designs, mirrors, and pictures. In a household, competition existed among its nuclear families and particularly among co-wives for the best room decoration. The outside walls of the house were decorated with bright, bold, colorful designs, including such modern symbols as airplanes, trains, and ships as well as desert animals and insects, birds and palm trees, stars, the sun, and the crescent. These drawings and decorations had magical significance. For example, drawings of scorpions and snakes on the front walls and doors were believed to have the power of stopping these creatures from entering the house. Other drawings, such as the sun and a big eye were painted to neutralize the harmful effects of the evil eye, belief in which constituted one of the important, common supernatural beliefs among Nubians. Other drawings represented the means of transportation used by the *hagg* (pilgrim) in travelling to Mecca; pilgrimage was highly valued among Nubians.

The Nubians' love of homeland and pride in their character and community make them, when away from their villages, stick together and help each other. In cities, several Nubian associations have been established on both regional and ethnic bases. In 1920, to reinforce a sense of common identity and to protect their interests as a minority group, Nubians formed a club in Cairo and another one in Alexandria. Membership is open and encouraged for all Nubians regardless of their linguistic or ethnic background. While the Nubian associations have traditionally provided a place for gathering and entertainment, they also performed social duties such as in cases of death and marriage. The two Nubian clubs have established the role of representing Nubians before official circles. They basically assume a political role in addition to other social and sports activities. The associations and the two clubs serve as channels of communication between Nubians at home and those at work in cities. Nubians who chose to settle permanently in cities continue to be concerned about news of their original homeland in general and their villages in particular. They very often participate in the club's activities; and, more important, they render services for newcomers to the city and help them find jobs and settle down.

In her observations and reflections on Nubian society, Hohenwart emphasized what she considered a unique trait of community spirit among the Nubians: "I often asked myself how the Nubians could endure the hardship of life during these last fifty years. And then I found that they had an inner happiness which was reflected in the people's faces. Peace and serenity, cheerfulness and kindness, helpfulness and charity characterized this good-looking race. The precious gifts of nature were also gifts for the people which—we hope—they will preserve also in the new environment. Friendliness and mutual understanding are inherent traits which can be found in extended families, family-groups, tribes and all those people who possess a widespread community spirit. I am certainly not mistaken if I consider this community spirit to have been one of the most remarkable phenomena in the Nubian society" (1975:186).

In addition to this cohesive community spirit, Nubians have an unmistakable sense of history and originality. They always refer to the remaining antiquities in their land to emphasize their early civilization and their contribution to Egypt's ancient culture and glory. They often mention that Nubians had once gained power over all Egypt, ruling from 750 to 656 B.C. as the Pharaohs of the xxvth Dynasty. Nubians also say that the word *Nubia*, which means "the land of gold," reflects the richness of their land and the role it played in the formation of an ancient lavish civilization. Nubians are pleased with the continuity of traditional life as they put it. The rhythm of life has always been slow and relaxing. Gerster notes that "tradition has it that Christianity reached Alexandria in the middle of the first century; the new religion gradually replaced the old Egyptian gods. Islam conquered Egypt in the year 641, but Christian kingdoms lingered in southern Nubia for another 800 years. Nubia is a place where great changes have always come slowly; where neither the three Nubian dialects nor the Arab settlements scattered through Nubia have altered their identity; and where time—like the Nile—has seemed to have neither beginning nor end" (1963:594). How much change relocation can bring to traditional Nubian life and how fast such change can take place are two questions with which this book is concerned.

Chapter Two
Aswan Dams and the Nubian Exodus

It was ironical and sad that the impending destruction of Nubia was the occasion for many of us to get to know and appreciate Nubian culture.

Liala S. El Hamamsy (Fernea
and Gerster 1973:xii)

Aswan Dams

Egypt, as the ancient Greek historian Herodotus observed, is the gift of the Nile. It was the intelligent and careful use of the Nile waters that made possible ancient Egyptian civilization. Modern Egyptians also turned to the Nile for more water control and utilization to meet the demands of progress. When Mohammed Ali Pasha seized power in 1848 and aspired to make true his dream of a modern country awakened following long ages of backwardness, he turned to the Nile to transform its water into wealth through a network of irrigation projects. His goal was to extend the cultivation of cotton, an export crop that suited the country's soil and weather. Capital in hard currency would then be available to import Western technology for industrialization. But the Pasha's great hopes for an industrial development corresponding with an agricultural expansion were blocked under the British rule that followed the 1882 invasion (Fahim 1981).

The British wanted Egypt to remain essentially agricultural, with a possible increase in cotton cultivation, which they viewed as having the highest economic returns. More water, however, was needed for an increase in cotton planting. In 1902, the construction of a dam was completed across the Nile a few kilometers south of the town of

Aswan, forming a reservoir with a storage capacity of up to 980-million cubic meters of water in an artificial lake extending south for a distance of about 140 kilometers. In subsequent years, however, the Aswan reservoir seemed unable to meet the growing demand for more water to make land extension feasible as well as able to support a steadily growing population living in limited arable areas. Egypt's population was 7,930,000 in 1882, had become 11,190,000 in 1907, and reached 14,178,000 by the 1927 census; while the total cultivated area was 4,758 feddans in 1882, 5,374 in 1907, and 5,544 in 1927 (Waterbury 1977:2). This marked an increase in the population size of nearly 43 percent in less than half a century, while the amount of land under cultivation increased only 14 percent for the same period.

As a result of an apparent growing need for more water to cultivate new lands, the Aswan Dam was heightened in 1912 and again in 1933. A third increase of the reservoir capacity seemed necessary once more in the 1940s, especially when the population reached nearly 16 million and satistics showed a steady decline in both the per-capita cultivated and cropped areas (from 0.60 feddans in 1882 to 0.33 in 1937 to 0.31 in 1947, and from 0.72 feddans in 1882 to 0.53 in 1937 to 0.48 in 1947, respectively [Waterbury 1977:3]). This measure was, however, not favored in engineering circles due to its questionable long-term effectiveness. Instead, British hydrologist H. E. Hurst developed the idea of a huge reservoir that would store enough water for an entire century, thus saving the people from famine and the land from inundation, which had resulted from low and high floods, respectively. Because he viewed the Nile as a geographical unit— and the projects for its full development as also forming a unit, the parts of which must work together—he concluded that the location of the new reservoir should be in Lake Victoria, one of the main sources of the Nile.

This same idea of large-scale, long-term storage was also taken up by Adrien Daninos, a Greek-Egyptian agronomist, who proposed having the new high dam erected at Aswan instead of the Lake Victoria site. The new vast reservoir would, according to Daninos, take care of everything: annual storage over the years and protection against low and high floods. Neither of these two proposals was put into effect, however, until the Egyptian revolution broke out in July 1952, and a solution to the persistent economic problems became imperative (Fahim 1981).

One of the stated goals of the revolution was the elimination of the social ills of a long-standing land feudalism. According to Waterbury, "In 1952, a small minority of 2,136 owners were in possession of 1.2 million feddans, 20 per cent of all cultivated land at an average of 560 feddans per person. Conversely, 2.6 million owners, 94 per cent of all freeholders, possessed only 2.1 million feddans, 35 per cent of the total for an average of 8 feddans per owner (1974:4). In September 1952, revolutionary Socialists promulgated land reform laws, which limited land ownership to 200 feddans per person and redistributed the confiscated lands (about 20 percent of all cultivated land) among exploited farmers. The limitation and redistribution of feudalistic lands actually reflected a social reform measure rather than an overall solution to economic problems. (Later, in the early 1960s, land ownership was reduced to only up to 100 feddans per person.) In the new search for answers to Egypt's economic hardships and the revolutionary aspirations for providing a better standard of living, history seemed to repeat itself when Egyptians again turned to the Nile for a solution. The search resulted once more in an engineering project designed to cope with human problems; the idea of erecting a new dam at Aswan was therefore seriously discussed and adopted before long by the Revolutionary Council in November 1952, only a few months after the revolution broke out.

The Aswan Project was perceived by the Revolutionary Council as very promising, particularly in terms of adding new arable lands, increasing the output of the existing cultivated lands, and generating the electrical power that would promote the advanced level of industrialization Egypt has long striven to achieve. Perhaps more importantly, the Daninos Aswan Project appeared to accomplish Hurst's century-storage notion within the national borders of Egypt. His idea of using the African Great Lakes for a reservoir site was disregarded primarily because of the possible dangers of water-control politics resulting from the involvement of several partners with conflicting interests.

Although there may be more than one thousand registered high dams in the world (defined as those above 75 meters in height), no similar dam has attracted as much worldwide concern, publicity, and controversy as the Aswan High Dam. Some, like W. H. Wisely, former president of the American Association of Civil Engineers, described it as "a modern engineering wonder fulfilling a vital need for the country's increasing population living on limited economic resources" (1972:37). Others, like Clair Sterling, a persistent critic of the dam, whose series in *The Washington Post* and leading scientific magazines have actually misled many Egyptian and foreign circles, perceived the dam as "a disaster reflecting a classical case of ecological ignorance and shortsightedness" (1972:86). Nonetheless, in reviewing the literature on the Aswan High Dam and related problems, the ecological side effects and their implications in the short run seemed to receive much attention and were also subject to conflicting views (Fahim 1981).

Four major dam-related problems were commonly identified and debated: (1) the water loss through seepage and evaporation; (2) the sedimentation of Nile silt in the lake and its impact on land productivity, sardine and brick industries, and the subsequent degradation problem; (3) the water-logging of soil and the high level of soil salinity from year-round irrigation; and (4) the disease menace in increased schistosomiasis due to the extension of irrigation. In general, official government reports often emphasized the point that these problems may exist, but they did not constitute a potential threat to the positive contributions of the dam. As in other projects that cause substantial environmental changes, government publications and most newspaper articles often argued that the side effects had been anticipated and could be handled on a scientific basis rather than by unqualified and unjustified antagonism to the dam and its national value. Foreign reports, mostly from the West, however, argued that the dam's side effects constituted serious, complicated problems and had been given too little attention in the past. (For further information see Waterbury's book [1979] on the hydropolitics of the Aswan High Dam.)

On the basis of several assessment studies conducted by national and international experts during the 1970s, such as the joint research project between the University of Michigan and the Egyptian Academy for Scientific Research and Technology, the Aswan High Dam seems to have achieved to date its main goals in terms of water storage, hydroelectric power production, and water management. This provided Egypt with the potential for further agricultural and industrial development. Nevertheless, the environmental impacts of Lake Nasser (the reservoir) and river flow controls have caused a variety of social, economic, and public health complications. Some of these effects were anticipated during the planning stages, while others were not. As of 1980, Egypt was designing and implementing alternative measures and water development scenarios in order to meet existing and potential future problems.

RESETTLEMENT AND NATIONAL POLITICS

Just as few dams are built without conflict, the Aswan High Dam was no exception. In 1954 Egypt requested loans in hard currency from the International Bank for Reconstruction and Development (referred to later as the World Bank), whose experts had studied the Aswan Project and found it "technically and economically sound" (M. Heikal 1973:52); but the United States, after an initial endorsement of the project and willingness to share in providing the bank's loan to Egypt, declined. The withdrawal of the American offer, although officially attributed to economic reasons, was politically derived due to Egypt's involvement in the nonalignment movement of the 1950s and her conflict with Israel. This incident, however, engendered controversial views and interpretations.

Whatever the motive may have been, Egypt felt hurt and obliged at the same time to proceed with its development plans. Consequently, the late Gamal Abdel Nasser, then Egypt's president, nationalized the Suez Canal on July 26, 1956, in order to use its hard-currency returns for the construction of the dam. As a reaction to this move, the British, the French, and the Israelis invaded Egypt in October 1956. The invading troops that occupied Sinai and the canal zone were compelled by world pressure and a United Nations resolution to pull out only a few months later in December 1956. That withdrawal, however, did not end the political complications related to the construction of the dam. In 1958, Egypt accepted a Soviet Union offer to help finance and construct the Aswan Project.

Consequently, Egypt took the Aswan High Dam Project as a serious challenge and mobilized its resources. Any critical discussions of the dam's potential dangers to the environment were often taken as an act of national treason. Although the government was quite aware of certain adverse ecological effects, the general tendency was to emphasize, and sometimes dramatize, the project's assumed positive contribution to the realization of the country's national aspirations, especially in the areas of agricultural and industrial development. Within this conceptual framework of the dam, the resettlement component of the Aswan Project was conceived as a sizable and manageable social cost. Nonetheless, the Egyptian government showed apparent concern for compensating the Nubians for their loss of a homeland and therefore determined to plan for a successful resettlement scheme.

Nubians and the Two Dams

Two dams are presently erected across the River Nile south of the city of Aswan, located approximately eight hundred kilometers south of Cairo. The people who were most affected had always been the Nubians; yet the effects of the new dam, i.e., the Aswan High Dam, cannot be compared to those of the old one, known as the Aswan Dam or Reservoir. While the impact of the first dam was relatively limited in terms of the amount of land inundated and the necessity for the displacement of several villages away from the reservoir, the second dam's effect was total, flooding all Nubian lands within the Egyptian territory and nearly one-third of the Sudanese Nubian Valley. All Egyptian Nubians and those Sudanese affected by the new lake (fifty thousand people on each side) had no alternative but to leave their homeland. In his book, *The Nubian Exodus*, Hassan Dafalla, the man who was assigned to relocate the Sudanese Nubians from their homeland to a new site, perceived the situation as follows: "However great the benefits of this agreement [referring to the 1959 water agreement between Egypt and the Sudan] the side effects were disastrous. The Nubians were the only victims as the greatest part of their country was being doomed to inundation. In Sudanese Nubia, the town of Wadi Halfa and twenty-seven villages with all their agricultural land, date trees, and historic remains would be swallowed by the waters" (1975:6).

The two Nubian groups, in Egypt and Sudan, to whom the border dividing the Nubian Valley into two halves was a political line rather than a cultural boundary became separated and experienced totally new lives under different resettlement schemes. Egyptian Nubians were relocated in the Kom Ombo region, a new site still in the same Aswan region, while their Sudanese fellows were taken to an area about eight hundred kilometers away from their homeland and situated in a rather unfamiliar climatic, ecological, and cultural environment. This is the Khashm el-Girba area, in Kassala province near the Sudanese-Ethiopian border.

The Nubians have always felt that the two Aswan dams drastically upset their traditional life and placed them, against their will, in an unfamiliar and uncertain existence. Following the construction of the first dam and its subsequent raisings, Nubians—especially those whose lands were inundated—perceived themselves as victims of the dam and eventually became inflicted people, or *mankoubeen*, in their own term. The new dam intensified that perception and extended it to other Nubian groups. It caused them to suffer from depression and grief, especially experienced among the elderly. An educated Nubian provided a diagnosis for such common feelings when he stated that his fellow Nubians suffered from what he termed "a dam complex." According to him, the first dam forced Egyptian Nubians to leave their "beloved" land and seek work in the "unfriendly" cities where they never felt at home; but the second dam was a total curse which ended a life-style that satisfied their basic needs and gave them peace and happiness. Labor migration had split families and created communities where females outnumbered males. The outcome was quiet Nubian villages dependent on cash remittances and patiently awaiting the return of absent men.

Sociologist Peter Geiser (1973), however, frees the dam from the responsibility placed on it by the Nubians and suggests that they have built what he calls "the myth of a dam," which functioned as an adaptive mechanism for the conflicting feelings of their love and attachment to their native land and the necessity throughout their history to seek work in the cities. Geiser argues that there is historical evidence indicating that labor migration, as a mechanism to cope with limited resources, had existed among the Nubians long before the construction of the first Aswan Dam. The first dam, however, increased its scale and forced many Nubian families to settle permanently in cities or leave Nubia in groups and establish new communities in the rural areas of the Aswan region. In addition, writers are skeptical regarding the amount of truth in the feelings expressed by the Nubians relative to their native land, and believe they are presenting an exaggerated form of grief over their loss.

The archaeologist Rex Keating is one of those who feel that attachment to a native land is natural, but finds it difficult to explain why it is particularly strong among the Nubians. Their land, he writes, "offers nothing of wealth, little comfort, so poor was it in economic resources, in particular, arable land, that they were compelled to pass a large part of their working life in cities in order to support their families at home in Nubia." Yet, he also writes, "always with advancing years, they would abandon the attractions of the big cities, Cairo, Alexandria, and Khartoum, where most of them worked, to seek the simplicity of their homeland" (1978:38).

Another observer of the Nubians in their old setting, Anne Hohenwart, also wondered about this paradoxical issue of the poverty of a land and the contentment of its inhabitants. However, she found an explanation and writes: "The environmental attributes which were found here [Nubia] resembled those of other desert lands and riverain cultures: the river meant the stream of life, the supplier of water for man and cattle, the fertilizer for grazing grounds, for crops and trees, and the only way of communication. But the difficulties on one side allowed facilities on the other. The Nubians' life was more or less free and independent. They enjoyed their country full of beauty and silence. They loved their houses and extended compounds which were inherited within the same tribe from one generation to the next. They were proud of their historic knowledge. The Nubians, especially the older people, like to speak of former times, when the crops were rich and the palm-groves overloaded with dates so that the harvest satisfied the need of the people. The middle generation had felt the ever-increasing scantiness because fields and trees died away in the floods. The youth, however, became confronted with the hopeless situation hearing day and night that Nubia had to be given up for the sake of a better life in the near future" (1975:185–86).

RESETTLEMENT SURVEYS

Following Egypt's decision to implement the Aswan High Dam Project, the Council for National Development carried out preliminary surveys in 1957 to determine the potential flooded area and to obtain basic information on the villages to be affected. This survey revealed the physical difficulty and the high cost of resettling the Nubians in new villages on the lake shores beyond the expected 182-meter water level, so the Council urged the search for another site. In 1958 the High Dam Services Committee, in conjunction with several concerned ministries, chose the Kom Ombo site for the displaced Nubians and listed the responsibilities for each involved party. Also, because sufficient statistical information on the displaced people was urgently needed for resettlement policies and planning, the Committee commissioned the Ministry of Social Affairs to carry out a base-line socioeconomic survey of all the Nubian villages and inhabitants.

Subsequently, the Ministry of Social Affairs recruited research experts to design a schedule to obtain demographic information on the displaced Nubians and to carry out an appraisal of property, land, and animals. It also solicited opinions from the Nubians regarding the choice of the new settlement site and the policy of compensation. A one-month survey was carried out in 1960, covering 16,066 Nubian families in 535 *naja*s. Sixty social workers, with the help of 165 local school teachers, participated in data collection. The survey committee in charge was stationed on a steamer travelling along the Nile to supervise data collection. The staff recruited for supervision of data collection and checking was briefed in a two-day workshop held January 20–21, 1960. Data were processed in the Department of Statistics, tabulated and presented to planners for consideration.

ARCHAEOLOGICAL AND ETHNOLOGICAL STUDIES

At the same time, the Egyptian government also exerted every effort to preserve the Nubian monuments from submersion under the huge reservoir. UNESCO became involved and launched an international campaign to dismantle and remove the antiquities in Egyptian Nubia, with various countries assuming the responsibility for their removal and restoration. This international appeal for subscriptions to save the threatened artifacts, which dated back to the Upper Paleolithic era (17,000–12,000 B.C.), met with an enthusiastic response from several countries. The two temples of Abu Simbel were unique, and their removal and resurrection at the new location above the lake water level was indeed an engineering feat.

"It is somewhat ironic," wrote Walter Emery, the late British Egyptologist, that "the successive irrigation projects which have in the past destroyed, and in the present are destroying the antiquities and monuments of Nubia, are to a large extent the reason for our knowledge of the archaeology and history of this part of the Nile valley; for were it not for the periodic threat of destruction, there would not have been the concentration of archaeological research undertaken at various times since the Aswan Dam was built in 1902. Exploration in Nubia is difficult by reason of its isolation and, moreover, in comparison with Egypt the results of excavation are not rich in actual finds, although productive of valuable scientific information. Consequently, much of the archaeological exploration was the result of dire necessity and not of choice, and a large part of the important discoveries was made under threat of 'now or never' " (1965:15). But, contrary to several archaeologists who decried the damage the Aswan High Dam would bring to Nubia's historical treasures, Emery argued that the potential benefits of the dam and the new resources of the lake were enormous, and could not possibly be sacrificed in the interests of historical and artistic treasures.

Along with the vigorous concern for saving temples and other Nubian antiquities, there was a similar concern for recording Nubian culture before the inevitable change that would occur as a result of migration. In 1960, for example, the Ministry of Culture invited twenty eminent artists and writers to visit Nubia and provided them with a large boat on which to sail down along the Nile. The trip's purpose was to let each artist or writer record the area in the manner he chose. To preserve pictures and plans of the Nubian houses and villages that were outstanding for their variation of design and richness of decoration and architecture, a photographic survey was carried out. These works were widely publicized and received national attention and appreciation.

In addition, and in order to learn about contemporary Nubian culture, to record Nubian traditions and customs, as well as to seek insights and guidelines for resettlement planning, the Ministry of Social Affairs, jointly with the Social Research Center of the American University in Cairo, began a three-year project to obtain an ethnological record of Nubian culture and society. Under the direction of Robert Fernea, an American anthropologist at the University of Texas, Austin, the Social Research Center started "The Ethnological Survey of Egyptian Nubia" research project.

Resettlement Policies and Administration

As reported in a 1964 publication by the Ministry of Social Affairs in Egypt, planning for the Nubian resettlement program and its execution was assigned in 1962 to the Joint Committee for Nubian Migration under the chairmanship of an Undersecretary of State in the Ministry of Social Affairs. This committee was composed of representatives of other concerned ministries, and assigned a particular role to each ministry and coordinated the execution of these roles. It also recommended the establishment of an administrative Bureau of Development for the resettlement administration.

This administration started with a number of high-caliber administrators whose main responsibility was to provide the Joint Committee with information, insights, and guidelines that would help in formulating the resettlement plan. Resettlement personnel were recruited from different departments of the Ministry of Social Affairs, and their numbers increased as did resettlement activities. The multiple responsibilities of the resettlement administration necessitated the establishment of five administrative units in addition to two supervisory and coordinative offices in Aswan and Cairo. In brief, the resettlement plan included two stages: first, resettling the inhabitants of Nubia; and second, providing housing and social services for the *mughtarabeen* group, those Nubian emigrants who were already settled outside Nubia and wished to join their families in the new site.

The responsibility for evacuating the displaced Nubians, their settlement in Kom Ombo, and the financing of the entire project was shared by several government departments, each concerned with a specific task like housing, agriculture, health, and education. Total cost was then estimated to be in the neighborhood of 35 million Egyptian pounds. Overall responsibility, however, resided in the office of the governor of Aswan province. This made the Nubian resettlement project an integral part of the decentralized government program of economic development in Aswan province. Toward the promotion of a successful resettlement program, the government also considered the difficult conditions under which the recruited personnel were working, and, consequently, it rewarded them by a salary increment that ranged between 30 and 50 percent of their base salaries.

In 1960, both Egypt's president and vice-president visited Nubia to
show further official and national concern for the Nubians and to
assure them a good relocation plan and a promising future at Kom
Ombo: "The benefits which the Nubian people will enjoy are very
great. They will be brought together on a proper basis to build a
strong and healthy community. This will eliminate the complaint of
isolation and neglect. We are members of one family and we will
bring you together" (translated by HMF from Arabic; president's
speech to Nubians, January 1960). "If the Nubian people are leaving
their smaller home of Nubia for the prosperity of the republic and
the realization of the great hopes pinned on the High Dam, then the
bigger home, their own country will open its arms to welcome them
in one of the new districts in Kom Ombo. There they will find stability, prosperity, and a decent life" (translated by HMF from Arabic;
vice-president's speech to Nubians, January 1960).

In general, the Egyptian government gave the resettlement scheme
special consideration, intending that the process of relocation be
accomplished smoothly and successfully. However, there was no direct
Nubian participation in the government's formulation of plans. The
resettlement scheme was entirely organized and executed by the various ministries. Nonetheless, for two years prior to relocation a government committee for the investigation of Nubian demands held
monthly meetings with Nubian delegates in an effort to answer
questions and calm their fears. The Nubian voice was taken into
account whenever possible in order to accommodate Nubian desires,
as is the case in keeping the old names for the new villages in Kom
Ombo. Some Nubian leaders and representatives were also invited
to inspect an architectural model of a home before construction began
on the site.

Along with this policy, Nubians were also asked whether they
would prefer the Kom Ombo area or to settle where they could accommodate themselves. The results of the 1960 social survey overwhelm-
ingly showed that the common desire among Nubians was to go to
Kom Ombo, an important sugarcane and industrial center about fifty
kilometers north of Aswan on the east bank of the Nile. Two excep-
tions were the villages of Tomas and Afia, whose inhabitants differed
among themselves about where to go. One group chose the Kom
Ombo settlement and another decided to join relatives who had previ-

ously resettled themselves in 1934 in the area of Isna following the 1933 raising of the Aswan Dam. When I visited with Nubians of this group after relocation in 1966, they expressed satisfaction with their choice.

In regard to compensating Nubians for the loss of their land and properties, the government's policy was particularly sensitive. The goal was to have a fair policy that would satisfy the displaced people and placate their fears and complaints. Nubians were anxious about an equitable arrangement because, in their opinion, they had been previously cheated and swindled in 1902 and again in 1933 when the old dam was raised and they were compensated for their inundated property. Thus, Nubians were consulted on the type of compensation they were to get, the majority preferring to have it in cash. The government arranged for half of the money to be paid in cash while the other half would be held until the cost of land and housing for the new site was finally settled. The balance due was to be covered in installments over a forty-year period.

Several channels of communication developed and expanded as resettlement officials spent more time travelling along the Nile from one area to another and from village to village, gathering information and discussing the displacement operation. Administrators reported the Nubians' reactions and views to concerned authorities. These personal contacts were supplemented by information in pamphlets and radio broadcasts, answering many questions that arose involving the transition, especially those regarding property compensation and provisions for allocating new property and housing. Thus, it would be fair to say that there was direct, broad, and constant consultation and communication between the Nubians, especially their leaders and representatives, and the policy makers. Nevertheless, despite the government's sentiments and efforts, the Nubians' suspicions regarding the government and their future were not totally dispelled.

Chapter Three
Leaving Nubia on Noah's Ark

*It is more than their land that you take away from the people,
whose native land you take. It is their past as well, their roots,
and their identity. If you take away the things that they have
been used to see, and will be expecting to see, you may, in a way,
as well take their eyes.*

A passage from *Out of Africa*
by Isak Dinesen (1972:375)

AMBIVALENT FEELINGS

In the mid-fifties, when nationwide talk concerning the construction of a new high dam began, the Nubians realized there would be
an immediate impact on their lives, and expected to see more of their
land inundated beyond what they had already lost. A further move
inland would be required; perhaps affected areas would have to be
deserted entirely. When word was passed that they would have to
abandon all their villages along the Nile Valley, they believed it to be
a rumor that could not possibly be true. However poor their homeland might have been, the Nubians had struggled through their long
history to manage and maintain an existence in their valley. At first
they could not believe that "something would ever happen to take
Nubia away from them or move them away from her." However,
despite this attitude, which was gravely expressed by an old Nubian
with tears in his eyes, the decision to build the dam was eventually
put into effect in 1958. Nubia quickly became a scene of unprecedented activity; the inhabitants then realized a drastic event was about
to affect their lives and future.

39

As the difficult transition began, the Nubians felt hopeless in losing their beloved land and helpless with grief and depression because they had no alternative but to leave. Faced with the necessity of leaving their homeland, Nubians expressed ambivalent feelings. They had always viewed their land as blessed and considered its soil, climate, and water superior to that found anywhere in the Nile Valley. They loved the cleanliness, peacefulness, and personal security of their villages, while, on the other hand, they disliked the geographic isolation, which resulted in both material and social disadvantages (Fernea and Kennedy 1966:350).

Although most Nubians seemed to share this general ambivalence to some degree, the attitude toward resettlement varied according to several factors such as age, sex, urban experience, and economic security. The older generation, especially those who had never left Nubia, felt threatened by an urban way of life, which they generally pictured in terms of unfavorable stereotypes disruptive to Nubian customs. To allay such fears the resettlement administration emphasized its appreciation of the Nubians' sacrifice for national interests and its intention to preserve Nubian values and traditions in the new location. In June 1963 Hekmat Abou Zeid, then the Minister of Social Affairs, addressed the Nubians, saying, "We appreciate Nubian traditions and respect their spiritual and moral values. We want you to preserve and maintain them in your future life" (translated by HMF from Arabic).

Young Nubian men, especially those with urban experience and some education, seemed optimistic about the move. They looked upon resettlement as an excellent opportunity for establishing "a modern Nubian community" by gaining access to the different government services and breaking down the long-standing isolation from modern life. Their attitude was compatible with the government's plans to incorporate the new Nubian community into the regional scene as a more productive group. In addition, Nubian youths had hoped that with the new facilities and opportunities they would have new roles to play and, consequently, could achieve a higher status in the country. They wished to maintain their ethnic identity, yet be able to have greater participation in political and social life both regionally and nationally.

Married women favored resettlement in the hope that they would have more secure lives in which their husbands, then at work in the cities, could join them as economic opportunities became available. Widowed and divorced women looked at the move as going from a closed community to an open one where chances for remarriage would probably become greater; and mothers hoped that would be the case, for marriage is strictly endogamous. Although there are cases of intermarriage, it is on an extremely limited scale.

Absent husbands, working in the cities, favored having their families close enough for more frequent visits, although they feared the lack of safety and security for their wives and property in an area surrounded by strangers. People of the northern section of Nubia were much in favor of migration, perhaps because of their land, which, in addition to its limited size and productivity, had always been adversely affected by flood waters. But in the southern part of Nubia, where life had been better and the inhabitants had been the least affected by the old dam and its two heightenings, the general mood was one of depression. The new dam was viewed as destructive to a peaceful and pleasant life. Those with vested interests, such as boatmen, merchants, and border smugglers, resented the resettlement and spread ugly rumors, creating anxiety for both the Nubian community and the resettlement administration.

THE PRE-EVACUATION PERIOD

In March 1963 the government scheduled a final count of the displaced people; the continuous flow of Nubians journeying back and forth to work in Cairo made it difficult to estimate the exact number of people to be transferred to the new site. When this news was publicized, many Nubians residing in the cities rushed to the area, individually and in groups, to lend sympathetic support and solidarity to their kin at this time of distress. Many visited their dead, while others came simply to say farewell and visit Old Nubia before it disappeared under the water forever.

Others, however, came in order to take advantage of a situation that promised some government benefits, and eventually the resettlement administration had to limit entry into Nubia to only those listed in an earlier survey in 1961. This decision was resented by the Nubians, who described administrators as "heartless and cruel people."

A reporter describing this incident wrote, "This was an unsympathetic decision, but it seemed the only solution possible" (Horton 1964:16).

During the two or three months preceding relocation, in the summer of 1963, both the Nubians and the administrators were engaged in numerous activities. Administrators distributed cash compensation and settled over four thousand complaints. The Nubians were compensated for lost property, and those whose income was disrupted as a result of relocation were entitled to a monthly cash subsidy of up to five Egyptian pounds and eight Egyptian pounds until the first crop was harvested. This figure was based on an estimated per-capita annual income of rural Nubians prior to resettlement of about forty Egyptian pounds, compared to ninety pounds for Egypt as a whole.

As the time of the move approached, the administration assigned representatives to help familiarize the people with what to expect in the new location. The representatives distributed pamphlets in question-and-answer form for the literate people and also depended on information being circulated verbally from one group to another. In discussing the necessity of relocation and its benefits, administrators depended on an Islamic appeal favoring migration as a way toward a better life, and quotations from the Qur'an were cited.

In order to dramatize the Egyptian government's concern for the Nubian people, the minister of social affairs and a group of top government officials twice visited a number of the villages to inspect preparations for the move. The administration also depended on the help of the community as the southern villages were preparing to relocate. During my second visit to Nubia, I found almost all of the houses in the southern region bare of windows, doors, and even roofs. The land had been left uncultivated; the Nubians had cut down trees to produce charcoal and had untied the large wooden *sakias* (waterwheels) to sell as wood or to convert into charcoal.

In many Nubian villages, particularly in the northern section whose population was the first to move, people began to dispose of their livestock by selling or eating them. This practice increased, especially following a widespread rumor that the government had reached a decision to not allow the Nubians to keep their animals even after a one-month period of quarantine. Along with this decision people were encouraged to sell animals to the government as a preventive measure, considering the possible unavailability of fodder during the first year following resettlement. Many Nubians therefore disregarded the idea of leaving their remaining animals and poultry in the care of the administration when the death of quarantined animals taken from the first migrants was rumored. Instead, they devised illegal arrangements for the animals to reach the new land, either taking them on the move or transporting them over the desert mountain roads to relatives and friends in the city of Aswan to be sent later to the new area. Simple tricks, such as hiding small animals in belongings during the long journey to Kom Ombo, were often resorted to by the people.

FAREWELL TO A HOMELAND

The first displaced group was evacuated on the 18th of October in 1963, from the Kenuz village of Daboud, twenty-five kilometers south of the city of Aswan. According to the Ministry of Social Affairs report of 1966, this move involved 501 families, comprising 1,233 people including their personal belongings and livestock. Observers on the scene described that on the day they boarded the boats, the women rose at dawn to sadly and silently visit their dead, spraying the graves with water expressing compassion and sanctification. Visits were also paid to the *naja*'s shrine to show devotion and seek blessings. These shrines were the sites of pilgrimages and feasts that centered around the saints' cults. Devotion was traditionally expressed in the form of gifts or services to these shrines associated with holy men.

Observers were touched by the shared grief at the moment of departure. Many Nubians kissed the land as they left their empty, vacated homes, while others filled their pockets or small bags with soil. After boarding the boat, the Nubians were feeling particularly vulnerable and sat in deep silence, staring at the disappearing village; some had tears in their eyes and others cried openly. One Nubian, reflecting on the trip from his village down the Nile, which took him to the city of Aswan, said, "As we were sailing, I recalled Noah's ark. The boat was crowded, filled with personal belongings, poultry, animals, and pets. We were all heading toward the unknown." The administrators who accompanied the relocatees attempted to ease the shock and anguish of the people. Children and young people were encouraged to drum and sing. Informants reported that the facilities on the boat were excellent, with plenty of food and adequate medical care.

At the pier in Aswan, a warm reception awaited the first group of relocatees. First to welcome them was the minister of social affairs accompanied by a group of officials; and to symbolize the national concern for their displacement, representatives from the various public sectors came with bands and flags to greet them and to express the appreciation of the entire nation for their sacrifice. Following this welcoming ceremony, the Nubians then proceeded to the new land in the Kom Ombo region, travelling on comfortable buses while their luggage was shipped by trucks, reaching the new village shortly after their arrival. Official cars led the caravan of passengers, and, at the village of New Daboud, the first phase of settlement was carried out under the personal supervision of the minister of social affairs and several government officials.

At Kom Ombo

The relocation of this group had been successfully completed, and each family received a key to the new house. The warm reception and the efficiently organized move overwhelmed this first group of migrants from Daboud—so informants said. Porters helped them move their luggage into the new houses. A local market and a bakery were already functioning, and the resettlement administration was working hard to prepare the schools, clinics, markets, and other public services for full operation. A few days after the settlers arrived, the prime minister, on his way to Aswan to receive another group of migrants, visited New Daboud to investigate any problems that might have arisen.

Nonetheless, evacuation soon lost its initial image, and a crisis emerged. Despite the care lavished on the first group, the relocation of other Nubian groups was plagued with problems, the principal one involving poor scheduling of the moves. For example, a Kenuz village reported that the moving date had been postponed ten days, although a definite schedule had been promised. Due to a shortage of materials, some of the contractors had not met their deadlines in building new houses, and others had hurried construction, causing serious defects in the walls and roofs. Consequently, the administration postponed the departure date indefinitely (Abdel Wahab 1964).

In this instance, the Kenuz's belongings were packed, the windows and roofs from their homes had been removed and sold, and the livestock had been slaughtered or disposed of. Shops were closed, food supplies dwindled rapidly, and famine became a definite possibility. The result was widespread confusion, the people suffering from re-occurring bouts of depression that resulted from a state of transitory shock and depersonalization. The neighboring villages, seeing the plight of the Kenuz, organized and helped their fellows in order to avert disaster and to enable them to function on their own until they were able to be transported. This reaction was one of the first defensive resolutions exhibited by the Nubians in confronting a stressful situation without the help of the government.

In order to meet the urgent engineering deadlines at the dam site, the administration was forced to move people to unfinished houses in the villages. Construction of housing had not yet been started in some areas and, understandably, many Nubians felt the government's promises had been misleading and unreliable. Even when things went more smoothly, subsequent groups complained about the administration's neglect in providing them with an organized and official reception equal to that of the first evacuees. The relocation period took nearly nine months, from October 1963 to June 1964, and except for the good accommodation experienced by the first relocated villages, evacuations became ordinary routine work under the supervision of a committee whose members represented involved governmental departments.

Two main problems faced the resettlement administration during the implementation period. One problem was caused by inadequate communication among involved governmental departments due to bureaucracy and centralization. The other problem emerged directly from lack of synchronization between evacuation schedule out of Nubia and the engineering work at the dam site, which forced the Nubians at times when the rising reservoir water became threatening to leave Nubia and arrive in Kom Ombo to live in tents or temporary lodging facilities. Despite the government's concern and plans for a successful resettlement scheme, domestic and international politics in the early 1960s diverted all attention and mobilized the country's construction resources to work on the dam site and the diversion of the Nile into its new course on January 9, 1964, a date that was set for Egypt's president, the Russian prime minister, and several other dignitaries to officially inaugurate the construction of the Aswan High Dam.

A Lesson Learned

The Nubians had boarded "Noah's Ark" with great expectations but when they landed in "the promised land," it was not as green and convenient as they were told. The disappointment and grief were overwhelming. Because of that state of affairs, numerous and complex problems emerged and put both the government and the Nubians in a difficult situation. In retrospect, had the infrastructure work on the resettlement site been designed and implemented within the framework and construction responsibilities of the dam project, I presume that much trouble might have been avoided. I reached this opinion in view of the resettlement component of the Kpong Hydroelectric Project across the Volta River in Ghana (1975–81). The company contracted to construct the Kpong Dam was also responsible for the design and implementation of resettling some seven thousand people. This was done in collaboration with the government, while the World Bank assisted by providing funds and periodic appraisal missions. Although the company had problems with delays in land clearing and village construction, it was able, however, as a result of inspection and coordination with the government to catch up and meet the deadline without mishaps.

The differences between the Aswan and Kpong projects are obvious in terms of both the magnitude and the political implications. Notwithstanding, it seems reasonable to suggest the necessity of choosing the best arrangement in getting the relocation site at least in good shape, if not entirely completed, prior to the arrival of displaced people. Whether governments decide to have one or several companies in charge, alternative plans must be conceived should the construction fail to meet deadlines. Construction arrangements often vary from one setting to another due to many factors, such as cost, resources, and the location of the resettlement site. Nonetheless, if the Nubian case has a lesson, it is that planning and preparation for resettlement in all its stages, i.e., before, during, and after the physical displacement, determine the success or failure of this human challenge. Dam politics may be justifiable and rewarding at certain times; in the long run they can also have serious social and economic costs.

PART II

CULTURE CHANGE AND COPING STRATEGIES

Externally imposed, sudden and pervasive changes, as in relocation projects, produce considerable disruptions; and the social impact is usually enormous due to the large number of people who are relocated and the accompanying scope of the change. With resettlement the centuries-long life-style of the Nubians changed drastically. The shift from isolated and dispersed communities threatened numerous traditions, especially those related to village and family life. There were also significant changes in land use and farming practices, problems of food supply and distribution, consolidation of people into larger and more dense villages, and greater accessibility to social services and education—all of which paved the way for cultural upheaval.

Before leaving their old homes, as Hohenwart observed in 1963, "Nubians were determined to maintain their social system and keep their strong-mindedness." She presumed that, receptive to modern ideas and adapatable to new elements in their life, the Nubians might "stick to their traditional customs and obey their tribal laws so that honesty, firmness, and energy would ennoble their personalities in the future as it had been the case in the past" (1975:184).

Hohenwart's assumption has proved valid each time the Nubians have drawn upon their traditional culture to deal with the hardships of a new setting. Nonetheless, this has not been a unique Nubian response. On the basis of his intensive studies on people's responses to relocation, Scudder found that relocatees tend to cling to the familiar, changing no more than is necessary (Scudder 1973). This rather tradition-based behavioral response often occurs during a transitional period of multidimensional stress, which Scudder described as includ-

49

ing physiological, psychological, and sociocultural aspects. This state of inevitable stress can be expected to diminish only when the displaced people "regain their former self-sufficiency and develop a satisfactory relationship with their environment" (1973).

Like anthropologists, psychologists have also found that while not all changes disrupt, resettlement or community uprooting is particularly stressful psychologically. At the individual level, physical uprooting "disrupts, however temporarily, the sense of security and self-continuity of an individual moving through a changed physical and social environment" (Coelho and Ahmed 1980:97). Similarly, communities or groups under stressful change often have variations in their adaptive behavior within and across cultures, "for some individuals hurt more easily than others, some disintegrate more rapidly than others, and some recover and learn from severe crises of change more efficiently than others" (Coelho and Ahmed 1980:xvi). Nonetheless, according to the anthropologists Scudder and Colson, "people and sociocultural systems respond to forced relocation in predictable ways, predictability being possible because the extremely stressful nature of relocation restricts the range of coping responses available to the majority during the period that immediately follows removal" (1982:267).

Part II illustrates several types of stress, reactions to them, and coping strategies, referring to "the form of adaptation evoked under relatively difficult conditions or circumstances" (Coelho and Ahmed 1980:453). The conceptualization of the coping process is, however, much broader than what the term adaptation usually implies, and it is also discussed in omniscient and universal terms (Coelho and Ahmed 1980:471). Coping strategies, therefore, are to be viewed not only as instrumental means for dealing with the immediate psychological distress, but also as efforts to recover meanings (both structural and cultural) that may be irretrievably lost when humans are exposed to rapid environmental change (Coelho and Ahmed 1980:97).

In a speculative analysis of coping with forced migration and on the basis of a comparative study of the relocation experience of four groups (the Kreen-Akrore in Brazil, Mazatecs and Chinantecs of southern Mexico, the Chemahawin Cree in Manitoba, Canada, and the Bikinians of the Marshall Islands in the South Pacific), psychologist Joseph Trimble stipulated that "forced migration, as a type of migration and a process initiated by an agent external to the group *in question, inevitably contributes to psychological and sociological losses among group members. It also results in the loss of traditional, ancestral dwelling areas around which an entire cultural orientation and way of life was developed. Experiences generated by the relocation introduce an assortment of stressors, some of which are psychologically disturbing, but most of which are at least mildly disruptive. Stress reactions emerge and lead to the use of coping strategies to deal with them. As a consequence, the total relocation process is disruptive at a sociological level—familial patterns, role relationships and inherent responsibilities, forms of social control, subsistence patterns, and organizational structure are altered. Disruption at a psychological level occurs, too, affecting routine behavior, attitudes, motivation and emotion, and cognitive-perceptual styles. The interplay of the forces and structures at both levels therefore produces a complex state that may stabilize to the form it once was" (1980:468).*

When the displaced Nubians arrived in their new land in the Kom Ombo region, two crucial problems existed: one relating to the housing accommodations on the new site and the other involving the provision of new lands for the relocated farmers. However, these were not the only relocation problems.

Chapter Four discusses an important element of resettlement planning: housing. In an earlier draft of this chapter, I dealt with the housing issue in a general perspective as most relocation analyses often do, but this has now been changed as a result of an academic collaboration with Irwin Altman and Mary Gauvain. In a cross-cultural analysis, we have conceived homes as a tangible barometer of impact of social change on a culture and as an indicator of the mechanisms used by people to cope with change (Gauvain, Altman, and Fahim 1983).

Chapter Five examines the agricultural problems and assesses the viability of the economic base for the displaced community. One important virtue of the Nubian resettlement that the government repeatedly emphasized was the establishment of a new community with a very promising economic base where the need for male labor migration would be eliminated. Consequently, families would be reunited and enjoy a better life. Yet because of delays in land preparation and failure to provide sufficient new land holdings to relocatees at a satisfactory level, the labor migration that existed prior to relocation continued and expanded in volume and direction.

Another basic issue to be determined in resettlement planning is, according to Kurt Jansson, how settlers are to gain their livelihood. To what extent will it be from subsistence holdings and to what extent from production aimed at the market? Jansson argues that when governments devote scarce resources to capital-investment land reclamation and resettlement (as in the Nubian case), an economic return in terms of production for the market as well as for subsistence becomes mandatory. He further states that these basic institutional questions are "often not faced up to or are given low priority in most land settlement and development schemes in several parts of the world (1974:4-5).

The discussion in Part II concentrates on the notion of using old cultural ways to find solutions to emerging problems in the new setting of a life-style. The theme is also about change, especially those aspects relating to the rapidity and intensity of change. Some social changes occur gradually, while others take place abruptly and involve sudden alterations in settings and life-styles, as in the case of Nubian resettlement. In studying changes resulting from population displacement, the locus, pervasiveness, and extent of such changes should be investigated. These aspects of social change refer to the degree to which change affects vital and crucial aspects of a culture, e.g., the physical viability and well-being of people, the fabric of family life and social organization, or key elements of a culture's economic and political organization versus the degree to which social change affects relatively few and relatively superficial aspects of a culture. Thus, social changes may be pervasive and impinge upon central aspects of a culture, or they may have a limited impact in the breadth and depth of their influence (Gauvain, Altman, and Fahim 1983).

The source, rate, and locus of social change are probably not independent dimensions, and certain patterns tend to occur together. In a resettlement program, like the Nubian case, for instance, a government or external authority decides on a change, large numbers of people are uprooted all at once or over a relatively short period of time (such changes are always sudden for the people involved regardless of the length of time spent in planning and negotiating that may have preceded the change), and there are repercussions on many important aspects of life. In such cases it seems reasonable to infer that this confluence of factors associated with social change will have rather disruptive effects upon a culture. This pattern contrasts with that of internally generated, gradual, less widespread and central changes, where cultures slowly absorb practices of other cultures with effects restricted at any given time to only a few aspects of the traditional life-style. Here one might expect a less disruptive impact of social change, at least over the short term (Gauvain, Altman, and Fahim 1983).

As housing constitutes a basic element in the physical infrastruc-ture of the new site, community services are also essential, especially when they are provided as compensation for involuntary relocation. Chapter Six presents a brief description of government-provided com-munity services. It is interesting to note that the Nubians have responded favorably to the new community services and have actually taken some local initiatives in expanding them, as illustrated in Chap-ter Seven. While governments seem to succeed, in varying degrees, in improving social services in new communities, they often find it difficult to establish a viable economy for the displaced people. Failure, in most cases, is not only attributable to economic reasons. Whether for community services, economic viability, or the functioning of a resettlement scheme as a whole, it seems difficult to identify processes and assess consequences without studying carefully several interrelated variables, including sex ratios, population growth, ethnicity, and the relationship between Nubians and non-Nubian groups in the resettle-ment area. The relationship between the Nubians and the government also is an important dimension, if not a determinant, in shaping Nubian life now and in the future. The discussion in Chapter Seven, therefore, illustrates how in a resettlement setting diverse dimensions of interaction may emerge and certain coping strategies develop. It also calls attention to, hoping to raise interest in, several research issues that have been either poorly treated or totally overlooked in resettle-ment studies.

One of these research issues concerns resettlement and women. For a book on involuntary immigration and resettlement, Scudder and Colson researched the impact of relocation on women and concluded that, whether forced or voluntary, it "varies according to their socio-economic background, to their position in the household and to the society, and to the new context in which they settle" (1982:283). As to the Nubian case, I have found that despite overwhelming diffi-culties during the immediate years following resettlement, women have shown unusual capabilities to cope positively with stress. In general, resettlement has provided Nubian women with several options open to them in the Kom Ombo settlement, as well as in the cities across the country. Increased opportunities for education and employment are expected to expand women's involvement in Nubian community affairs, which suggests that change may occur in their lives more rapidly than among men.

Chapter Four
New Villages with Old Names

Four walls do not make a home.

Lagler (1969:12)

THE KOM OMBO RELOCATION SITE

New Nubia, or el-Nuba el-Gedida as it became known in Arabic, occupies a recently reclaimed, broad terrain on the eastern side of the Kom Ombo Valley, presently irrigated by reservoir water from the Aswan High Dam. The settlement design takes the shape of a crescent about sixty kilometers long, and is situated about three kilometers east of the town of Kom Ombo where the administrative center, known as Nasr Town, is located (Figure 3). The hot, arid climate of New Nubia differs little from the old setting, but the Nile, with its pleasant climatic effect, now lies from three to ten kilometers away. The sheltering groves of palm trees that were a distinctive feature of the old region, especially in the southern part, do not exist in the resettlement area. The rocky hills and sloping dunes that often separated the old Nubian villages from one another are also missing, and their lack is sorely felt by the Nubians.

Nubia today is no longer isolated from the rest of the country, as was the case in the old setting. The three ethnic groups are now settled in close proximity and have greater intensive social interaction than in the past. For ease of construction, and in order to facilitate access to the physical infrastructure and public utilities, New Nubia was designed as a compact area combining the 553 hamlets, previously dispersed along the Nile's bank for a distance of 350 kilometers, into

55

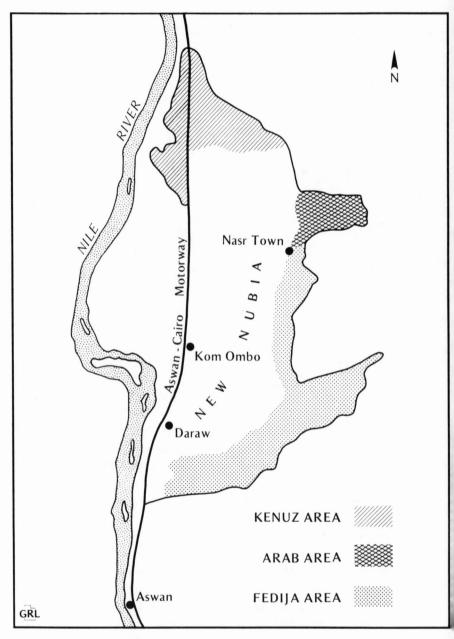

Figure 3. Generalized map of New Nubia.

forty-three large villages. These villages occupy an area of about two hundred square kilometers, including the new land that was reclaimed for cultivation. In this manner, the small, widely separated hamlets, each composed of less than one hundred residents, were replaced by densely populated and continuous settlements, nearly 25 percent of which contain a population of over two thousand.

The lodgings were symmetrically built in blocks to the size of the living quarters, varying from one to four rooms and including a limited area for a courtyard, kitchen, and bathroom. In response to the Nubians' demands the government assigned the names of the old *omedia*s to the new villages and placed them in the identical patterns of their native land. The government had planned a two-stage housing scheme for the Nubians. The first stage was devoted entirely to the housing for directly affected people; while the second stage, scheduled to begin following relocation, was planned for several thousand urban Nubians who at the time of the census for resettlement purposes were not residents of Nubia. Statistics collected in 1975 revealed that the number of completed homes for the first housing stage constituted 96 percent in contrast to only 2 percent for the second one. The main reason given for this discrepancy was the high cost of construction and the lack of enough space for additional building within village layouts.

The Home in Old and New Nubia

Since house design and function relate to a culture, it is worthwhile to examine the elements of relatedness between Nubian culture and the government houses. The interaction of these elements represents a form of adaptation or coping by a family, community, or culture to a new residence pattern. Gauvain, Altman, and I (1983) presumed a close relationship between homes and culture change and examined how factors associated with social change impinge upon certain characteristics of homes. Within this conceptual framework, Gauvain, Altman, and I attempted to demonstrate that social changes are often visibly reflected in homes and that the dimensions of openness/closedness and identity/communality can be used to describe some of these changes. The design, use, and modification of dwellings serve as a sensitive barometer of the state of a culture not only in times of stability but also during periods of social change. A comparison of the Nubian home before and after relocation illustrates this approach.

The traditional Nubian home was located within a small hamlet having a population of about one hundred people, many of whom were relatives and many of whom had lived in the community for generations. Individual homes were actually compounds that sheltered an extended family. The compounds were built about a quarter of a kilometer apart and, as a family grew, the compound was enlarged. For example, when a son married, he and his new wife often lived in a bridal area that was added to his parents' compound. In spite of the continued growth of a compound, some degree of separation and distance was always maintained between adjacent dwelling units. A family compound contained a guest area; courtyard; bridal hall; cooking, storage, sleeping, and living areas; an open, covered loggia or outside work area; and a stable for animals.

Openness/Closedness. The traditional Nubian home can be analyzed in relation to the dimension of openness/closedness. For example, the separation of compounds ensured that occupants could avoid interactions with others if they so desired. This was further aided by high (approximately 4–5 meters) and thick (approximately 0.3–0.6 meters) exterior walls. These walls were also important for temperature control since they enclosed high-vaulted rooms that were ventilated by numerous openings along the upper part of the walls. In addition, thick interior walls helped protect the privacy of household members from one another.

Other effective privacy-regulation mechanisms included the use of a single main entryway to the compound (a second entrance was sometimes added into the bridal-hall area) and the custom of not entering a compound without permission. In addition, a guest room for overnight visitors was always located to the immediate left of the entrance, away from the activities of the compound, thereby providing mutual privacy.

The traditional Nubian residence also had a number of design features that facilitated openness and social interaction. For example, the interior of the compound contained open shaded areas where family members could work or interact, and the guest room was often used as a family gathering place when there were no visitors. Also, directly outside the compound, attached to the front wall, was a bench-like sitting area, called a *mastaba*. Children often played on the wide *mastaba*, and adults would frequently sit on it and converse with neighbors and passersby. As such, the *mastaba* was a design feature of homes that enabled contact and openness among residents of the community.

Another way that people made themselves accessible to others was through decorating and painting the walls on the outside and inside of compounds. Individualized decorations, some of which depicted previous experiences, provided residents with a socially acceptable mechanism for revealing their accomplishments, skills, and interests to others. These examples illustrate how the traditional Nubian compound had a variety of means by which people could make themselves differentially accessible to one another.

The initial phases of relocation created a number of problems— settlement into densely populated villages, difficulties with food and water supplies, shifts in land distribution practices, inaccessibility to the Nile River, close contact between different ethnic groups, and so on. Of particular interest are the ways in which the new homes and communities violated traditional Nubian expressions of identity/communality and openness/closedness and thereby may have interfered with adjustment to the new setting.

In order to accommodate large numbers of people and reduce building costs, the New Nubian villages were arranged around straight, Western-style streets, with houses sharing adjoining walls. The shift from small, dispersed hamlets to large, almost contiguous villages resulted in far more contact among strangers and more noise, activity, and congestion than the Nubians were accustomed to. Homes in the new settlements varied in size and had from one to four rooms in addition to a small courtyard and a bathroom. People were assigned to homes according to the size of their nuclear families, which resulted in the fragmentation of traditional extended kin units. Along with the increased population density in the new villages, the small number and size of rooms in dwellings resulted in an increase in household density. In fact, household density doubled following the relocation (1.7 persons per square meter according to the 1966 census) and was associated with an increase in communicable diseases such as dysentery, measles, and encephalitis. As a consequence, mortality rates rose, especially for children and the elderly.

Traditional patterns of home design and use, which previously helped regulate the openness/closedness of household members, families, and neighbors to one another, were not available in the new communities. Fewer rooms meant that family members were forced to interact more with one another. The absence of a guest room often resulted in mutual intrusions by guests and the host family. In some instances, in order to provide a guest with privacy, a family would move in with a neighbor or kin. This arrangement was not wholly satisfactory, since it resulted in even greater contact between neighbors and kin than had been the case in Old Nubia.

Other features of the new home design interfered with customary practices of privacy regulation. For example, neighbors shared a common wall between dwellings, thereby eliminating a traditional barrier. Furthermore, walls around homes and the openings used for ventilation were much lower than they had been in Old Nubia, which made it difficult to maintain privacy. And, many new homes had windows in the front of dwellings, whereas in Old Nubia windows faced onto the courtyard and the outer walls had no windows or openings other than for ventilation. As a result of these new design features, passersby could easily hear household conversations and arguments. This led to strains in community relations as gossip heightened and as people had more than normal access to activities within a household.

The new dwellings also made it difficult to achieve desired contact with others. Extended kin and friends did not always live near one another, making it difficult for them to interact on a daily basis. This was particularly troublesome for women. Because of congestion, crime, and a general loss of feelings of security, women were no longer free to move about the community and exchange information with friends and relatives. They became restricted to their homes and were increasingly isolated from others and from activities in the community. In addition, the absence of a guest room led to less interaction with visitors, resulting in further isolation and loss of contact among people.

The absence of a *mastaba*, the low benchlike structure in front of dwellings, was another factor that affected social interaction in the new communities. It became difficult for people to interact with neighbors in a socially acceptable and informal way. If a person wished to sit in front of a dwelling he or she would have to sit on the ground. This behavior was frowned upon, however, because it was considered unclean and because it was a practice of Egyptian peasants with whom the Nubians did not wish to be identified.

Identity/Communality. The homes of New Nubia also affected many of the traditional channels used to express identity/communality. In Old Nubia, the ties of residents to their community and culture were evident in the widespread practice of decorating the exterior and interior walls of compounds and rooms. By means of paintings, carved reliefs, or decorative additions, residents displayed their bonds with the local community and with the larger cultures of Egypt and Islam. For example, elaborate and colorful paintings of the national flag symbolized bonds with Egypt; paintings of stars and crescents reflected adherence to Islamic principles, as did the special door decorations that symbolized the occupant had made a pilgrimage to the holy city of Mecca.

Common values and beliefs were reflected in paintings of hands, eyes, and other symbols, which were designed to protect occupants from the "evil eye" and other forms of harm. Such paintings appeared in different parts of the home, e.g., evil eye and protective symbols were drawn around entryways and living areas; scorpions were drawn near storage and water containers in order to protect the contents from contamination. Another common practice was to display china plates on the front facade of compounds as a symbol of the hospitality of the master of the household to the community.

In addition to community bonds, traditional Nubian homes depicted the individuality and uniqueness of the occupants. The paintings and decorations on the outside and inside walls of the compound displayed the distinctive artistic talents of their creators, who were usually women. Furthermore, unique aspects of the lives of the residents were often displayed: A steamship painted on a wall symbolized the fact that the owner had worked on ships; a carved relief of a man shooting an alligator identified the occupant as a noted hunter. Such displays not only reflected the unique qualities of the occupants but, as noted earlier, they also served as a vehicle for self-disclosure.

Decorative practices in the interior of the compound also depicted the unique identity of the occupants. For example, the guest room was kept very clean and decorated with wall hangings, handmade baskets, china plates suspended from the ceiling (these were also used for food storage), and elaborate articles of furniture. Much like the formal living rooms of the American suburban culture, the Nubian guest room displayed the unique talents, hospitality, and tastes of the hosts, especially the women. Other rooms in the courtyard were also decorated with handicrafts, souvenirs, personal mementos, photographs, and cherished family heirlooms that were unique to the occupants.

The new homes and villages violated many aspects of community bonds and inhibited expression of individual uniqueness. Because the new homes were small, it was difficult to adhere to Nubian values of cleanliness and tidiness, especially in relation to storage space and the maintenance of livestock. Consider the early months of adjustment in the typical new village: The Nubian people had moved from clean, well-decorated, spacious communities into high-density homes, communities with littered streets, housing with cramped interiors that had little room to store food and supplies, no place to keep animals (traditionally kept in separate areas in the compound), no guest space, and no room to expand. To solve some of these problems, dried food, fuel, and other materials were stored on the roofs of dwellings or were placed in the middle of streets. These practices proved to be frustrating and humiliating to the Nubian sense of group identity, however. Nubians traditionally distinguished themselves from the average Egyptian peasant, who stored belongings on the roof and kept animals in the home. To be forced to live as if they were poor peasants was an insult and an embarrassment to the Nubian cultural identity and self-esteem.

The sense of community fostered by the small hamlets of Old Nubia was seriously disrupted in the large villages, where there were many strangers and where people were separated from their extended kin and close friends. The fact that homes were built side by side and had common walls prevented the organic growth of the traditional compound, did not permit the housing of newly married children in the compound, and made it difficult to have a guest room. The extended family configuration and strong norms about hospitality to visitors, central features of the Nubian sense of community, were severely affected by the design of the new dwellings.

The design of the new communities and homes also interfered with traditional expressions of individual identity and uniqueness. Row after row of similar homes, the plain cinderblock construction, the disruption of status relationships regarding homes (e.g., landlords and well-to-do families lived side by side and in the same quality of housing as their former tenants and employees) all contributed to a loss of individual identity and self-esteem. The new homes had no decorations, were poorly constructed, and had no distinguishing qualities. To make the situation worse, the authorities prohibited major modifications of homes since many communities were considered to be temporary settlements scheduled for possible redistribution when the entire housing project was completed.

Nubian Response

Although the disruptions and stresses of the relocation were severe, the Nubians responded in ways that demonstrated their sensitivity to the importance of identity/communality and openness/closedness. Shortly after relocation the Nubians began to modify the government houses in accordance with traditional practices and in spite of government prohibitions. Although this may have been in part an intuitive and unconscious process, it was also often done deliberately. For example, one Nubian said, "If we want to maintain our old customs, we must maintain our Nubian architecture."

In some cases the traditional sense of community was reflected in cooperative projects. Streets were cleaned, and annexes were built to house animals. Groups of neighbors sometimes plastered the front facades of their homes, and in some instances neighboring families undertook cooperative decorating efforts in an attempt to make a row of homes appear unique and attractive. Many families began to paint the exteriors of their homes soon after relocation using traditional techniques and symbols. Paintings of Egyptians flags, the symbolic crescent of Islam, and decorations of honor were added to the fronts of homes. Residents also decorated the interiors of their homes. Floors were tiled; small rooms were added where possible to create an atmosphere of spaciousness; walls were painted with the traditional symbols such as scorpions, hands, eyes, and flowers. The color, design, and location of decorations varied by household, reflecting individuality, but traditional community symbols were present in many homes, especially in Kenuz villages where the traditional Nubian design of house architecture had been central to their culture and distinct to their ethnicity.

The Nubians also attempted to overcome features of the new homes that interfered with the regulation of openness and closedness.

Some families raised the height of the front walls of dwellings not only to achieve the traditional form but to permit greater privacy. In addition, low ventilation outlets were blocked and front windows were boarded up in order to restore privacy. Some families built a traditional *mastaba*, so that children could play outside and adults could sit in front of their homes and interact with others in the community. Many families also hung china plates over their front entryways—a traditional symbol of their hospitality and accessibility.

These renovations, although not done by everyone, illustrate how the Nubians attempted to incorporate traditional values with respect to identity/communality and openness/closedness in their new homes. To some extent they were successful in reproducing important facets of former practices in the new communities. But it was also the case that the expression of many traditional values was not possible, thereby setting the stage for permanent changes in the culture. For example, although the front walls of homes could be raised higher to re-establish privacy, side walls were shared with neighbors, and there was not always mutual agreement or resources available to make alterations. In addition, the cramped quarters and arrangement of homes in the resettlement villages did not allow for expansion. As a result, one community built a communal guest house to accommodate visitors. Although this solved the physical problem of housing visitors, it was not wholly satisfactory because of the impersonal nature of the arrangement.

Members of one family solved the problem of limited space by adding a second story onto their home. However, they were criticized by others because the side windows of the second story overlooked the courtyards of adjoining homes, thereby violating the privacy of others. The problem was resolved by closing and permanently locking the shutters of the windows that overlooked neighboring homes. Another family moved out of the residence area of the village and built a larger home. Although this arrangement provided more space and expressed individuality and status, the family was also isolated from the community to a greater extent than had been customary in traditional Nubian hamlets. In summary, although the Nubians were able to deal with certain problems associated with their new homes and communities, not all problems *could* be resolved.

RESIDENCE PATTERN, HOMES, AND CHANGE

A striking illustration of an immediate effect of the new residence pattern and homes on community life and cultural aspects has been apparent in some marriage and residence rules as well as certain ceremonies. For instance, in Old Nubia the married couple moved to the bride's place of residence; but this no longer applies due to inadequate space, and the couple must seek accommodation elsewhere. In cases where divorce occurs, many times the wife remains in the home because according to the government's relocation provisions the home belongs to the family not just the husband. This has resulted in numerous problems, especially since in many cases there is no alternative.

In terms of traditional ceremonies and practices, the Nubians, sensing the loss of their long-established cultural patterns, tended to substitute cultural values that had served a similar purpose in order to adapt to the new residential situation. Lack of personal space and the development of interaction among new neighbors, who in most cases were not kin, were two major factors that led the Nubians to restructure their religious ceremonies as a village affair rather than as a tribal practice. In some villages where the people were economically better off prior to relocation and thus received good compensation, guest lodgings for entertainment and social functions have been constructed. These lodgings serve for the various functions of receiving condolences and congratulations during cultural states of crisis.

Over the years immediately following relocation, there has been considerable simplification of several of the traditional Nubian ceremonies, especially those associated with birth, marriage, and death. In Old Nubia it had been the custom to extend these celebrations for many days in order to allow relatives and friends, including those working and living in the cities, to travel by boat from distant areas. The compact resettlement area with its relative closeness to the rest of the country, along with other factors such as inflation, economic hardship, and stress, obliged the Nubians to reduce the length of these ceremonies. Some informants worry about a possible negative effect in the long run on the spiritual qualities structured within the culture as they see ceremonies related to the biological crises of life radically changed and modified. Actually, since the establishment of New

Nubia, the traditional and complex festivities accompanying male circumcision were completely dropped by quite a few families just three years after resettlement. Death and postmortem rituals have also changed, ranging from complete cessation to simplification and reduction. For example, condolences to relatives of the deceased are held for only three days in contrast to the fifteen days of earlier times. As our data of 1971 show, the memorial services for the dead held at the cemetery four Thursdays after death, then on the fortieth day after death, and one year after death are no longer observed among most Nubians.

IMPLICATIONS AND CONCLUSIONS

The Nubian case is but one of several resettlement programs that illustrate how sudden and imposed social changes are reflected in homes and how they can be partially understood in terms of the dimensions of openness/closedness and identity/communality (see Gauvain, Altman, and Fahim 1983).

The resettlement of the Nubians created a number of stresses associated with the move itself—shifts in agricultural styles, food and water problems, and the general upheaval of the social structure. It also seriously interfered with the ability of people to regulate openness/closedness and identity/communality in the ways that had been customary in their traditional hamlets and homes. I can only speculate whether the stresses of relocation would have been reduced if the new homes had permitted appropriate expressions of cultural values associated with openness/closedness and identity/communality. The government houses in New Nubia impaired the ability of people to express themselves with respect to these dimensions, and therefore may have interfered with their adjustment to the new environment. I do not mean to suggest that the best solution to the Nubian case, or to other instances of resettlement, is to simply reproduce the traditional home in the new environment. Instead, our analysis (Gauvain, Altman, and Fahim 1983) suggests that environmental designers and planners should attend to the underlying sociocultural and psychological dimensions of identity/communality and openness/closedness when designing new homes and communities, especially in cases of sudden and pervasive social changes. The planner or designer, ideally in collaboration with residents, should address a number of questions relating to the new homes and communities: How are values associated with identity/communality and openness/closedness expressed in the traditional homes of a culture? What is the relative importance of expressing communality versus identity, or of openness versus closedness in the homes of a specific culture? What are the likely consequences if people are unable to express these values in the new setting? What compensatory ways does a culture have for exhibiting a particular value?

Answers to diagnostic questions of this type can serve as the basis for development of alternative designs for homes and communities. According to the logic of this chapter, it would be crucial to assess the degree to which various alternative designs are compatible with cultural values embodied in traditional home designs. The thrust of our analysis does not require the physical duplication of traditional home designs, which in fact may be difficult due to space restrictions, population density, limitations of technology, and a host of other factors. Instead, we call for functional equivalency between old and new homes. Efforts should be made to incorporate in new homes the functional capability for people to express cultural values associated with openness/closedness and identity/communality. In the Nubian case it may not have been physically possible to create large separate compounds in order to insure privacy. However, there may have been compensatory design features that would have permitted an equivalent level of privacy even though the physical setting was different.

A growing trend of indifference toward house structure and appearance may in part be attributed to the deteriorating environmental conditions in quite a few Nubian villages. For instance, lack of coordination between the housing and agricultural schemes resulted in certain villages, such as Dahmit and Adendan, being constructed on unsuitable sites. In this area the land is relatively level, sloping slightly from east to west toward the Nile's mainstream, which subjects the residents on the western side to serious drainage problems. Swamps have been and still are forming in several stretches of the terrain, creating breeding habitats for mosquitoes. This condition exists in nearly 20 percent of the new villages. Adendan has become totally unfit for human habitation and must be relocated elsewhere.

Another serious repercussion of the poor water drainage is the rapid filling of latrines, necessitating the constant removal of sewage.

I heard Nubians complaining of the cost and effort involved in cleaning the latrines, the delays in cleaning often developing into problems
among neighbors due to the offensive odors, water seepage, and the
accumulation of solid waste. Wash water is also thrown into the
streets, causing disputes among neighbors. Increasingly, these problems not only have become a nuisance for many people but, more
seriously, have created health problems.

In conclusion, it is interesting to note that much of what the
Nubians have done to their houses since relocation clearly reflects
different states of mind toward adjustment. Immediately following
relocation they began with changes in the outside appearance of the
houses to reassert their former distinct status as individuals. Later,
by the second or third year in Kom Ombo, they wanted to distinguish
themselves as a community from neighboring non-Nubian villages or
groups. Painting, remodeling, and decorating the interior of houses
came at a later stage in an attempt to settle down and "feel at home."
They, then, looked at the houses as "a property" that would give them
a feeling of belonging to the new place and provide them with a sense
of security in an unfamiliar land.

But as the years went by and the Kom Ombo settlement failed,
in the eyes of most Nubians, to become a viable community that could
provide a promising future, the Nubians tended to do less work on
their houses even in terms of maintenance. Those who can afford to
save money or who obtain regular remittances from either working
husbands or children in oil-producing Arab countries, invest not in
the house structure but in the home furniture. They upgrade what
they already have and buy new items, mainly appliances, which have
become status symbols, and families compete over what they have
inside their houses rather than how the house looks. When informants
were asked why, the common answer reflected a hopelessness in
improving conditions in Kom Ombo and a great desire to leave.
As one person clearly explains, "We can take our furniture with us
should we leave; why then should we care about the house which
we might leave behind?"

Also, during visits to Nubia in 1974, 1977, and 1978, I found a
number of the streets occupied by barns and littered with animal waste,

which attracted flies and frequently created a health hazard. The barns were built either in the centers of streets or in areas adjacent to the living quarters. Cleanliness, a distinct quality of the old villages, is fast disappearing in many areas where space can no longer accommodate both human and animal populations in compact areas.

Chapter Five
Making a Living at Kom Ombo

If the settlers' potential for development is to be treated as one of the most precious resources of a new settlement, it must not be countered by shortsighted governmenal measures.

Kurt Jansson, a United Nations
technical advisor (1979:8)

BACKGROUND

As part of a nationwide scheme of land reclamation and cultivation by using the Aswan reservoir water, approximately twenty-seven thousand feddans in the Kom Ombo area were allocated for Nubians. This constituted nearly one-third of the total new lands in the Aswan region. The Ministry of Land Reform had been in charge of reclamation projects until 1965 when a new government organization took over, the Egyptian Authority for the Cultivation and Development of Reclaimed Land (EACDRL). The delay in getting the new lands ready for the displaced Nubians resulted in the reclamation of only 10 percent of the allocated lands at the time of relocation in 1963.

Away from the Nubian Valley and the Nile, the Nubians found themselves in a land of "sand and stones," their great expectations of "a green land" based on the government's promises, unfulfilled—so they said. Rushed relocation, dictated by political objectives and dam engineering necessities, had not allowed for adequate preparation of the land. The arrival of some fifty thousand new settlers in an area of already limited economic resources created problems, and from the beginning the Nubians were unable to subsisit on the new land or

71

function from a viable economic base. Food shortages occurred and prices soared due to big demands and short local supply. The settlers searched in distant markets for fresh green vegetables, fruits, and fodder for their livestock.

A RESETTLEMENT FOOD CRISIS

The government, attempting to counter the food shortage and the exorbitant prices, made bread and groceries available in the local markets, but this measure proved inadequate to meet the Nubians' demands. Seventeen of the newly established bakeries were put into full operation to provide the settlers with bread, one of the basic staples of the Nubian diet. But, the Nubians found it unpalatable and gradually replaced it with their home-baked breads, which suited their budget and taste and which were necessary for the specific dishes included in traditional ceremonies. These bakeries, which were costly to build, were closed by 1971 with the exception of four, which functioned to provide bread for the government schools in the area where lunch meals were provided.

Groceries and canned food, including meat and fish, were also available in four of the state-managed consumer cooperatives, but the Nubians, used to fresh products, were dissatisfied with the price and taste of canned food and were unwilling to make it their staple diet. Abdel Wahab (1964), reported that when the Nubians from the villages first searched throughout the cooperatives for olives, white cheeses, and *halwa* (a sesame sweet), which can serve as a whole family meal at minimal cost, they found instead only the expensive and unfamiliar canned foods.

While attempting to cope with the food problems in various ways, the women, traditionally responsible for domestic expenditures, resorted to the old patterns in developing inexpensive means to supplement and diversify the family diet. Quite a few planted small vegetable gardens to compensate for the shortage of green vegetables. These gardens were created by mixing alluvial soil into the sand in the courtyards or in front of the homes, and they were irrigated with water from the public facilities (Fernea and Kennedy 1966). This practice continued despite official efforts to prevent this use of the relatively limited, potable water.

The Egyptians government, as a result of the delay in getting the land ready for distribution and cultivation, had to urgently request relief in the form of food commodities from the United Nations Food and Agriculture Organization (FAO). The distribution of FAO commodities started one year following relocation and lasted for eighteen months, from January 1965 until June 1966. During this period, displaced families lived on a minimal government subsidy, determined by the size of the family, and received food aid in return for a nominal cost deducted from the subsidies. About 60 percent of the total number of resettled families received these subsidies, and the remaining 40 percent made their living through means other than agriculture, such as domestic work in major cities or clerical work in Aswan's government departments. This expenditure, officials explained to me, added substantially to the resettlement budget.

In assessing the relocation food crisis and its implications for individuals and community health, it is important to point out that Nubians did not by any means reach a state of starvation; yet, the food situation was very unfavorable on both health and social grounds. For several months before relocation, Nubians, as part of their preparation for the move, ceased cultivating their lands and consumed their animal and grain stock. In some instances, when departure schedules were postponed, the food situation was reported to be extremely bad. As a result, there were Nubians who were actually undernourished long before they settled in the new land. Insufficient and inadequate food in the new locality resulted in further malnutrition among those people. Doctors found that the food crisis affected health conditions among the relocatees at a time when they needed to be physically capable of coping with relocation stress.

Doctors also reported that protein deficiency was evident in the Nubian diet. Resistance to infectious diseases was described as very low, especially among infants and elderly people. Official vital statistics show a high rise in the crude death rate among relocatees during the two years following relocation, from 13.6 per thousand in 1963 (the year preceding the beginning of relocation) to 23.6 in 1965 (the year following the completion of relocation). This substantial increase in mortality, in spite of improved medical facilities, is a possible consequence of the food crisis and its complications. Besides, the lack of adequate food over a long period created a state of anxiety among the relocatees due to the uncertain prospects of life in the relocation area and aggravated what Fried labelled "the grieving for a lost home" (Fried 1963).

LAND DISTRIBUTION : POLICIES AND PROBLEMS

Not only did the Nubians come to a land unable to accommodate them, but they were also subjected to two stages of land distribution. In 1966, only six thousand feddans, nearly one-third of the land under reclamation, became accessible for distribution. This land was distributed among the most needy families on the basis of one feddan per family. But the size of these plots actually varied between 14 and 21 *kirats* (one feddan is equal to 24 *kirats*, or 1.038 acres). Also the Nubians received half of the allocated land in a nearby site and the other half in a distant location with a poorer quality of soil.

As to livestock, the relocation authority had transported about three thousand head of cattle to New Nubia, some of which died shortly after arrival. Shortage of adequate fodder combined with change of habitat caused the general health conditions of the cattle to deteriorate. The government arranged for each landholder to receive one cow, whose price was to be collected in long-term installments. In addition, many Nubians bought one or more cows from neighboring local markets depending on how much money they had as a compensation for their lost property in Old Nubia. The government made it possible for cultivators to purchase a cow on a five-year credit plan at an interest rate of one percent.

According to information obtained in March 1979 from EACDRL, nearly 19,465 feddans were distributed among 10,406 out of the 16,300 remaining displaced families by that year. The new land was thus finally distributed among approximately 60 percent of the relocated families, which consisted of three categories of Nubians: those who had previously owned land and cultivated it themselves; those who had owned land, but had not been farmers; and those who had not been landholders, but were agricultural laborers.

Nubians in the first and second categories were allotted as much land as they owned prior to relocation up to a maximum of five feddans per family. Those who previously owned more than five feddans received cash compensation, while the landless Nubians of the third category were allotted two feddans per family. Paradoxically, however, those Nubians who owned less than one feddan in Old Nubia were not included in land distribution, but were instead compensated in cash for their loss. These Nubians protested this provision as "unfair"; they wanted to be considered landless in order to receive the two-feddan allocation. However, there was no possible way to accommodate their demands due to the lack of arable land in the resettlement site.

In addition to problems of land compensation, there was resentment expressed among the people regarding the conditional food aid. This involved the second stage of food aid in 1970, which was distributed as an incentive for the landholders to farm. If they chose not to accept the assigned land, they could not receive aid, and this created great displeasure over what the Nubians called "the agony of land distribution." The seriousness of the land distribution issue was evident when many Nubians filled the drainage canals with soil in order to expand their field area. These problems developed into uneasy relationships between the farmers and the administrators, which resulted in individual, and sometimes tribal, conflicts. Concerned over the repercussions of the land distribution policy and associated problems, a Nubian leader expressed his fears to me in 1971 of the "possible adverse effects regarding the Nubian community over a long period, for land distribution was already creating local tensions and jealousies between close relatives and long time friends and neighbors."

The new land, like the old, lies in an arid, rainless zone and depends upon water transported from the Nile for irrigation. This water is lifted by power pumps from stations into three main canals, and flows from the canals to several branches, where it pours into field channels with central regulating gates. Unlike the situation in Old Nubia, where water was lifted from the Nile by means of manually operated pumps and ox-driven waterwheels, the new fields are watered by the free-flow irrigation system except where the land is higher than the water level.

This new method of irrigation caused numerous water drainage problems for the land and dwellings adjacent to the course of the main canals, and in certain areas, due to flooding, settlers were forced to evacuate their homes and leave the fields filled with drainage water. The gate-irrigation system has created frequent disputes among neighboring farmers because of its inefficiency, the common neglect of careful timing, and the allotment of irrigation water it releases. Individual irrigation disputes have flared into family and tribal quarrels, causing a further nuisance for the administration. In addition to these problems, many Nubians are often reluctant to supervise night irrigation for fear of being harmed by devilish creatures, known as *aman doger,* which are believed to emerge from the Nile or any body of water and wander over the land during the night (Kennedy 1970).

A more serious, and possibly catastrophic, problem is waterlogged soil with a high salinity resulting from year-round irrigation and too much water being constantly shunted onto the land. In Egypt the problem is especially severe because the Aswan High Dam's ample water supply, combined with the hot climate, enables the land (which previously produced one crop per year) to yield two or three crops, and so irrigation continues unceasingly. Also, due to inadequate drainage systems, the water sits in the blazing sun evaporating and depositing salt in the soil.

A government commission's report described waterlogging as largely traceable to the delay in implementing adequate drainage schemes, to the wasteful use of irrigation water, and finally to the practice of perennial irrigation—the continuous application of water, which affords the soil no rest. As of 1980 serious considerations and measures were in the process of planning and implementation to solve these problems.

FARMING PRACTICES AND MANAGEMENT

In order to integrate the Nubian economy with the regional sugarcane industry, each settler is required to cultivate sugarcane on 40 percent of his land unless the soil is sandy or otherwise unsuitable. As growing cane on such a large scale was not widely practiced by the Nubians before relocation, they lacked sufficient knowledge and practical experience to do the work properly. The government, therefore, provided them with technical and administrative supervision and accepted the responsibility for marketing the crop. In addition to sugarcane, Nubians cultivate some traditional crops, the most important of which are cereals such as wheat, sorghum, and barley. The government does not intervene in marketing these crops; assistance is limited to the provision of seeds, fertilizer, and necessary agricultural equipment on credit.

Thus, land cultivation and management have been state-directed through the establishment of cooperative societies. All landowners are, by law, members of government-supervised cooperative societies directed by an elected board of landholders which serves as a liaison between the farmers and the administration for agricultural management and services. The functional importance of the cooperative societies to the economic rehabilitation process raises the question whether it is realistic, in non-Western countries, to designate management responsibility to the farmers when their previous experience has not included large-scale management. This would seem impractical, especially in the context of an agricultural resettlement program that conforms to the regional sugarcane industry. The existing problem may be viewed as resulting from the incompatability of two opposing systems: the first, the agricultural setting in which the farmers work; the second, the ideologies imposed by the government.

While the involvement of farmers in the management of their own businesses was the ideological base for the organization of agricultural cooperatives, Nubian leaders frequently argue that they are actually denied freedom in the decision-making and action processes. Administratively, each cooperative has an elected board of directors under the supervision of the agricultural bureau that is responsible for the cultivation of the reclaimed land in the Kom Ombo region. Two administrative members, one being the agronomist in charge, also serve on the board; and it is significant to note that while none of the agronomists are Nubians, ten out of the fifteen agricultural aides working in the cooperatives are. The overall proportion of Nubians working in the cooperatives is approximately 54 percent, although most of them are engaged in clerical work.

My observations in 1978, and administration reports of 1979, indicate that Nubians showed a relatively more positive response toward the state-managed sugarcane cultivation than they had earlier. Yet, local variations do exist among the three ethnic groups as a result of their past knowledge and experience in agriculture. For example, the Fedija of the southern part of Old Nubia, known as settled farmers with better experience in agricultural work, have satisfactorily continued their cultivation practices in the new settlement. In terms of cane cultivation, the Fedija land produced the highest output, averaging 21 tons per feddan in the 1977 season. In contrast, the Kenuz, who had little or almost no recent experience in farming, have been in some villages a source of trouble to the administration. Excuses such as the poor quality of the land and the inadequate system of irrigation have often been used by the Kenuz to justify their failure in meeting the administration's expectations. In the 1977 season, the sugarcane yield was an average of 11 tons per feddan. As to the Arab group, whose lands were last to be reclaimed and redistributed, it is still early to pass judgment on their farming ability. In the 1977 season, they cultivated only 1.3 percent of the total sugarcane land area of eight thousand feddans.

Agricultural development seems to be substantially affected by a clash between two subcultures: the land development agency and the displaced community. Administrators, relying on their long experience in dealing with peasants in the rest of the country, soon discovered that they had overlooked some distinctive characteristics of Nubian history and cultural traditions contributing to an atypical agricultural background. Unlike Egyptian peasants, many Nubians, for historical and cultural reasons, are neither eager nor willing to work a piece of land of their own. Those who have agricultural land prefer to be landlords rather than tenants. The traditional pattern had been Saiydis for labor, while a resident family member managed the land for the absent owner. (*Saiydi* is an Arabic term for the inhabitants of Upper Egypt.) Nubians want to resume that pattern in their new setting regardless of the administration's opposition. Their attitude toward land cultivation has greatly hindered agricultural policy because many Nubians are not doing their own farming or are unable to produce as much as anticipated.

Another cultural factor affecting the attitude toward working the land was the marked incidence of working Nubian women. The Nubian migratory pattern of men flocking to the cities had resulted in a large percentage of women not only assuming the responsibility for family welfare but also engaging in agricultural pursuits. In the years prior to relocation, the 1960 census showed the working population composed of about twelve thousand persons in Old Nubia, nearly one-third of which were women. But while women composed nearly 5 percent of the total working population in Egypt, the National Research Center of Cairo in 1959 counted the number of working Nubian women as 14 percent of the total working population in Old Nubia. This discrepancy does not alter the fact that the majority were engaged in agriculture in order to "keep the valley green," as the Nubians say. In the new community, women are not allowed to work, with the exception of older women who, due to a lack of economic security, work only when close to the villages.

The enormous cost in money and time necessary to complete the technical aspect of land reclamation and cultivation is an additional complication affecting the Nubians' motivation, commitment, and capacity to meet the government's expectations regarding production. This production, according to the most recent statistics of 1979, has steadily increased; yet these statistics can be misleading if we interpret them as an indication that Nubians have become more involved in agriculture. This is not the case. On the contrary, the Nubians have drawn upon the old system of sharecropping to solve the problems of maintaining the land while continuing to pursue their jobs and professions in the cities. Once again, they have adopted this method as a compensatory measure, but it is no longer practiced, as before, between relatives. It has evolved into a system dependent on contacts between the Nubians and the Saiydis. Now it is primarily the economic interest that binds the relationship and affects the Nubian motivation to maintain the land. This factor as well as the census of 1976 demonstrate a Nubian out-migration from the resettlement area and are indicators that the Nubians, mostly from the Kenuz and Arab groups, have not adjusted to the role of settled farmers.

The government's plan to incorporate the Nubians into the economic mainstream of the region has not proved successful. These people, with an independent trait characteristic of their culture, have not been able to conform to the agricultural structure that involved almost total intervention on the part of the government. The changes have come too quickly and without adequate consideration for the Nubians' aspirations or their motivations for achievement. During interviews, I frequently questioned them regarding their ambitions for their children; and, although many of them were employed in the cities as servants or worked the land as farmers, nearly all of them wanted their children to have the opportunities for a better education and to aspire to the higher professions. One of the factors affecting this attitude has been the change in the value placed on the land. In Old Nubia, land was limited to the green valley, and its value was determined by the quality of the soil (dependent on silt deposits from the Nile) and the availability of water. The land in New Nubia is reclaimed desert, and water is sometimes scarce. This factor has devalued the land and affected the Nubians' relationship with it.

The land distribution policy allowed for a standard ownership of two or five feddans, which eliminated land as an object of status and deprived the Nubians of this long-enduring factor in their social system. They lost the sense of belonging, attachment, and commitment to the land. The fact that the Saiydis, formerly their hired laborers, had also obtained land adjacent to their property, served to depreciate the value Nubians place on land ownership. No longer do the people desire to rise socially or economically through agriculture; and the consequences have been extremely costly, not only to the Nubians, but to the government as well.

The government's viewpoint is that the land, which was expensively reclaimed, should be cultivated, and its land reform policy precludes absentee landholders. Farmers are obliged to cultivate their land themselves; otherwise, it will be taken from them. Nubians, however, had previously managed their lives in a way that provided for the cultivation of land but did not specify that the owners cultivate it themselves. They also prefer to make independent decisions concerning their land and its cultivation and interpret the government's agricultural policy as an inappropriate intervention into their personal business.

On several occasions the agricultural bureau, committed to delivering the sugarcane crop to the Kom Ombo factory no later than a specific period, had no alternative but to cut the cane in areas where Nubians did not observe the scheduled dates. The bureau then charged the negligent or reluctant farmers labor costs. I therefore always looked with reservation upon the official figures of increased land production (up to 30 percent in some areas) as an indicator of more Nubian input into sugarcane cultivation. The point is, as a senior official told me, that the government would not tolerate seeing the expensively reclaimed lands neglected or left uncultivated. "Green land," he emphasized, "must remain so whether Nubians do the job or we have to do it."

Related to the effects of differing attitudes toward agricultural development is the problem of ineffective communication. Official records show that 53 percent of land recipients are women, most of whom do not speak Arabic. (Land was registered in the name of women whose husbands were absent during the pre-resettlement survey.) Traditions do not allow them to meet with strangers to discuss business. Instead, male relatives substituted for them in dealing with administrators or hired laborers. In addition to the language and sex barriers, the administrators' attitudes and efforts are often misinterpreted. This is clearly exhibited by Nubian resentment toward the government-appointed agronomists whom they view as "ignorant supervisors" on matters about which Nubians assume they know better. Government-initiated suggestions or regulations are often taken as orders and are strongly resented.

Misunderstandings due to lack of effective communication expanded the barrier to smooth collaboration between farmers and administrators. Administrators have reported that any dispute between an administrator and a farmer usually becomes the concern of the latter's tribe and sometimes his entire ethnic group; the whole group will then suspect the administrator's motives. Ethnic group rivalries further annoy administrators, who are often accused of favoring one group over another, as in cases of agricultural land distribution.

Differing assumptions and expectations have also contributed to the complexity of the confrontation between administrators and Nubian settlers. One important administrative assumption implicitly underlying development plans was that the Nubians would do what traditional farmers would have done in a similar situation, while the Nubians have a different experience of and attitude toward farming. Also, the administrators expected appreciation and gratitude from the settlers in return for efforts to better their socioeconomic conditions. However, to the administrators' surprise and displeasure, Nubians justify their attitude by the belief that "development is a right and not a favor" because they were forced to leave their homeland; accordingly, the government is obliged to satisfy their demands. While the administrators have national objectives in mind, settlers are more locally oriented in their outlook. Paradoxically, Nubians who have become administrators are often accused by the other settlers of ignoring Nubian interests in favor of government goals.

One main goal of resettlement and rural-developmental plans was to raise the relocatees' income through the cultivation and development of newly reclaimed lands. While officials report an increasing income among those farming the lands, the Nubians have always claimed that they are not yet economically self-sufficient. But when would they consider themselves economically independent? When asked this question, Nubians can provide no reliable answer; however, in 1971 they complained to me about the disappointingly meager return from the land. Many view sugarcane cultivation as unprofitable and claim that sometimes they end up with debts. They would rather cultivate their traditional crops. The administrators always point out that if the Nubians would do the agricultural work themselves instead of hiring laborers from neighboring communities they could make a profit. The Nubians maintain that their labor input in agriculture cannot make up for their earnings from city work. EACDRL tried to survey production and monetary returns, but this was unsuccessful, apparently because either the interviewees declined to respond or they gave false information. I also failed in 1975 to get such information when administering an interview schedule to a sample of Nubian farmers.

ABSENTEEISM IN NEW NUBIA

Because there were delays in land preparation and failures to provide sufficient new land holdings to relocatees, labor migration did not cease as was anticipated. To accurately determine the volume of absenteeism is, however, difficult due to the lack of periodic statistics on population composition and dynamics since 1966. The number of newcomers to the area is not recorded. Nubians are also reluctant to report villagers who leave, fearing the loss of government services and cash subsidies. Local administrators report that the phenomenon of male absenteeism from the new villages does exist, but its volume is not as high as it was prior to resettlement. They estimate about 20 percent of the male population are circular migrants. (In some parts of Old Nubia the number reached as high as 90 percent.) In 1973, I was told by the undersecretary of the Ministry of Land Reclamation that absenteeism would decline shortly as "Nubians learn how to benefit from farming and adapt themselves to the new setting."

The proportion of absentees to the total male population is probably much greater than the administrators' estimate although its volume varies from one ethnic group to another and sometimes from village to village within the same group. When I later discussed the problem with the undersecretary of the Ministry of Land Reclamation, he revealed that male absenteeism had actually reached nearly 50 percent in some Nubian villages. The 1976 census confirms this statement. In some Kenuz villages like Garf Hussein, Dahmit, Koshtamna, and Marwaw the sex ratio ranges between 38 and 50 men to 100 women. The Fedija sex ratio is 80:100 on the average, compared to 62:100 among the Arab group. However, 1976 data on sex ratio and land per capita indicate no correlation with emigration, contrary to the pre-relocation setting, as Scudder concluded from his sample study (1966:31).

The basic problem, however, is neither the amount of cultivable land nor its productivity, but rather the Nubians' traditional orientation toward city work. This does not at all imply a lack of interest in land use; but, as mentioned earlier, unlike Egyptian farmers, many Nubians do not wish to work their own land. Even without the land-pressure factor (although the arable land has reached its maximum limit), emigration would be expected to continue in New Nubia.

The increasing volume of absenteeism is clearly demonstrated by the sharp decline in the population size of New Nubia after an unprecedented increase of 2.5 percent during the two years following relocation (from 55,395 in 1964 to 58,303 in 1966). This substantial increase was most probably due to demographic and social factors such as the constant flow of people into New Nubia from the cities. In the 1976 census a decline of 1.5 percent in the population size was indicated, with the figure dropping to 56,916. This shift can most certainly be attributed to the absenteeism of migrant workers: The continuing migration out of Nubia extends beyond the cities of Cairo and Aswan into the oil-producing countries of Kuwait, Saudi Arabia, and also into Europe and the United States. In England, the Nubians have formed a club that meets with top Egyptian officials to discuss Nubian problems and the possibilities for the future. This club has been effective in channelling energy and money into Nubian enterprises, continuing, although far from home, to help the growth of its people back home.

The trend toward work abroad is growing due to the increased tendency among the Nubians to educate their sons. This has proved to be an investment in the future, for they are rising rapidly into the professions, accommodating themselves to the expanding job market. The main factor in this expanding migration continues to be the unusual system of job recruitment based on kinship ties and ethnic affiliations, which has facilitated the progressive transition out of the community while allowing individuals to maintain the ties that bind them to Nubia. After their long struggle to live in an imposed setting, the Nubians, by and large, have reached two alternatives, either to continue these migratory patterns in their new setting or to return to their old homeland once it becomes habitable (see Chapter Eight). This is how the future of the Nubians is shaping up after almost two decades of residence in the Kom Ombo settlement.

WHAT WENT WRONG?

Farming problems outlined in this chapter seem to coincide with the analysis by Gary Nelson and Fred Tileston. They conclude that "in most instances agencies have attempted to overlay a traditional culture with an extremely complex system or systems that are little understood by the traditional cultivators. The result is that the cultivator has little vested interest in running the system beyond his own head-gate and it is somebody else's fault when water does not arrive in proper amounts and in a timely fashion at his head-gate, and furthermore, he feels helpless to do anything about it. Also, since he is not directly helping to manage and run the system beyond his head-gate, the government or agency concerned must supply all the management staff and facilities necessary to operate and manage the system. This results in excessively high overhead costs that are one of the principal factors contributing to producing a non-viable activity" (1977:23).

The linkage between irrigation agriculture and traditional agriculture also presents another striking example of incompatibility. Irrigation agriculture, according to Nelson and Tileston, is an abrupt departure from traditional agriculture. It is a capital/management intensive production approach as opposed to more traditional methods. Moving into irrigated agriculture often requires double cropping in order to amortize the capital investment, thereby modifying the entire structure of the farmer's labor-requirements calendar. As a substitution for this system, Nelson and Tileston have suggested adding an "agricultural supplementary activity" to the existing traditional system rather than totally replacing it. They conceive such activity as allowing a much smaller hectarage per family, thus spreading investments over a larger primary group. It also appears to be more attractive to the farmers as it avoids putting eggs in an unknown basket. Nelson and Tileston also point out that the use of irrigation cultivation as a supplementary activity must be tested and explored as a first step in the development process, and minimum technology, including hand construction, must be encouraged in order to increase the potential of the projects (1977:24–25).

This proposed supplementary activity was eventually tried in the Nubian agricultural scheme by allowing the relocatees to continue their traditional agricultural system while maintaining a state-supervised cane cultivation on only 40 percent of the land area. (Irrigation techniques in New Nubia were different, of course, from those in Old Nubia.) This arrangement, however, did not meet the planners' expectations, and the agricultural development scheme has become one of the major sources of difficulties toward adjustment to resettlement. The Nubian experience suggests, in my view, that perhaps a major obstacle to the success of a resettlement agricultural program lies in the move of the relocatees to an area that is not yet ready to produce. And this is in addition to the delay between planting and matured crops. The result has been the creation of a dependent population and an intolerable situation where the relocatees very often become consumers much more than producers. In such cases, development of economic self-sufficiency and sociocultural self-respect becomes an illusion, never a reality. I conceive four major policy propositions that would promote proper functioning of resettlement agriculture: (1) a compatibility between the old and new agriculture systems as much as possible; (2) a gradual introduction of the new system, depending on the progress of relocatees in adjusting; (3) a reinforcement of positive motivation through an effective means of incentives and concrete, rewarding returns; (4) planning a community-based viable economy not just for the male head of the household, but also in terms of employment and investment for all of the family members both in farming and nonfarming activities. To achieve these four propositions as well as others that different resettlement situations may require, the issue of careful advance planning and effective management seems basic.

Chapter Six

Community Services and Change in Scale

Uprooting has to do with one of the fundamental properties of human life—the need to change—and with the personal and societal mechanisms for dealing with that need. As with the more general problems of change, uprooting can be a time of human disaster and desolation, or a time of adaptation and growth into new capacities.

John H. Bryant, M.D.
(Coelho and Ahmed 1980:xi)

BACKGROUND

In the previous two chapters, I presented information on land farming and housing and discussed their related problems. In this chapter I describe briefly the community services that the government had provided for the displaced Nubians at Kom Ombo. Also covered are Nubian responses to the new facilities, which far exceed, in quantity and quality, what previously existed in Nubia. Not only did these services introduce new or modern elements into traditional Nubian life, but they also brought about a change in scale, i.e., a change in the number of people interacting and the intensity of the interaction.

In her conceptual analysis of social change in Africa, Monica Wilson indicates that "there is general agreement among anthropologists about the reality of increase in numbers of people interacting: not only are formerly isolated societies drawn into wider relations, but there is cumulative increase in population. Both processes have been most conspicuous during the past four hundred years. Changes in the nature of interaction are more debatable. Durkheim thought that the

87

total amount of interaction increased: that people grew more and more dependent upon one another. It can be argued that the amount of interaction remains constant, but is more or less spread out, for as villagers begin to depend upon the world of strangers, they are less dependent upon each other, and on their kinsfolk in the same or other villages. But whether Durkheim or his critics are right, none doubt that people interact in wider and wider circles; that this applies to more people as education and travel become more common, no longer the preserve of clerics, or literati; and that trade with what were once remote villages swells. The increase in scale applies in time as well as in space" (1971:7–8).

INFRASTRUCTURE, COMMUNICATION, AND ENERGY

The differences between Old and New Nubia in topography and settlement pattern have been previously discussed. New Nubia occupies a limited area, and its villages are built in close proximity to one another. The land is a flat plain, relatively free of elevations and obstacles to the flow of water, the reverse of the situation in Old Nubia. The flatness of the land facilitated the construction of a network of roads connecting the villages with one another. The Ministry of Public Transportation has set up a bus line for travel inside New Nubia, thus replacing the small boats and donkeys, which had been used for short journeys, and the Sudanese Nile steamer, which used to sail twice weekly for longer journeys.

The villages of New Nubia are now connected by a circular road that is about forty-six kilometers long and opens onto the Cairo-Aswan road. Another twenty-three kilometers of roads connect the main road with the villages. A branch road, thirteen kilometers long, connects Nasr Town with Kom Ombo City.

The topography of Old Nubia not only made transportation difficult, thus isolating the villages from one another and from the rest of the country to the north, it also prevented an effective operation of postal services between villages. This situation changed with the move to the new settlement, where there are twenty-four post offices, or about one for every two villages, with each office serving about 2,431 people. The 1971 national average was one office per 4,297 people.

Telegraph and telephone services, extremely limited before resettlement, have become sufficiently available to all villages. There are twenty-five telegraph offices, or two for every three villages. Part of these services are run by the Nubians themselves as local agents. About 58 percent of the post offices and 68 percent of the telegraph and telephone offices were established and are managed by the settlers under the supervision of relevant authorities.

The provision of electrical service was very limited in Old Nubia, its availability confined to some of the main villages either because of their administrative function or because power was needed to operate irrigation equipment. In New Nubia, all streets and government buildings have electric lights. A number of inhabitants have succeeded in connecting the current to their homes by "unofficial" means. Electricity is expected to be available for every new house when the nationwide electrification project for all of rural Egypt is completed (probably in the mid-1980s). When this happens the consumption of electricity will increase, especially because of the additional number of radios, televisions, fans, and kitchen appliances that will be in use.

The energy resource issue is especially important in developing countries where a particular community may not consume much energy in the home environment due to close adherence to traditional living. Upon relocation, however, the newcomers to an established community become potential consumers of energy at the average usage rate of the individuals already living there. This prospect is also a factor to be considered in making any net energy computation to meet future demands of a new community of consumers. For example, prior to resettlement, the Nubians baked their own bread using wood for fuel. However, the seventeen bakeries built in the new homeland used fossil fuel to bake bread, making it a highly expensive food in terms of energy consumption. Other examples abound, such as the energy needed for water purification, pumps, transportation, new roads, etc.

Water and Food Supply

A network of two hundred public facilities for potable water has been installed in the new villages, with an average of five units per village. Each unit usually has four taps. The settlers themselves installed about 26 percent of the units. A large number of the facilities are not maintained properly, resulting in water leaks and the formation of waterlogged areas. In addition, the network of potable water draws its power supply from another network (in Daraw, about ten kilometers south of Kom Ombo), and very often the main network cannot support the water consumption of the branch system. This leads to a cutting off of the water supply, which sometimes results in problems.

Some Nubian villages frequently suffer from lack of water, and this constituted one of the major problems communicated to the minister of local government during his visit to the Nubian Club at Alexandria in June 1977. In this connection, Scudder noted that "it is one of the ironies of large-scale man-made lakes in Africa that several miles inland from the lake margin (the Nile in regard to the Nubian case) relocated communities are frequently plagued by inadequate supplies for themselves and their live stock" (Scudder 1975:462).

As to food supplies, the people of Old Nubia used to buy food from peddlers who travelled from place to place in small boats or from merchants living in the villages who usually bought their goods from Aswan or Wadi Halfa. There was also a store in most hamlets where food supplies and other basic materials were sold on credit until families received cash remittances from relatives working in urban centers or until they received the revenue from their lands. Nubian families used to stock up on necessary food supplies for as much as a year at a time. There were no consumer cooperative societies, such as existed in many other Egyptian villages, which could have supplied the Nubians with basic food supplies throughout the year at reasonable prices.

During the early stages of resettlement, the Ministry of Supply had been concerned about making different consumer goods and food materials available. To this end the Ministry set up nine wholesale consumer cooperative societies, four household cooperative societies, ten large markets, and twenty-two smaller markets. The large markets consist of a number of shops and storehouses as well as the consumer cooperative. The size of the market varies according to the area and the population it serves; the large market serves a group of neighboring villages and consists of fourteen to sixteen shops. The small commercial center serves one or two neighboring villages and consists of four to six shops.

The markets are not only places for buying food supplies, but are also centers where other domestic facilities are available. In 1972, the markets included 105 grocers, 12 cafes, 9 wholesale consumer cooperatives, 4 household cooperatives, 6 greengrocers, 4 butchers, 8 stores for miscellaneous small goods, 4 tailors, 3 carpenters, 3 plumbers, 5 barbers, and a number of restaurants and shops offering various other services. In addition, there were about fifty shops ready for occupancy but not yet rented.

In spite of the centralization of trade in these markets, commercial activity also extends beyond them, and it is common to find Nubians in the villages who have turned one of the rooms in their homes into a shop where they transact business in the traditional Nubian manner. Also, the idea of having "little malls" in the villages was not favored by the Nubians, who feared that the marketplaces would attract strangers and they would thus lose control on their own territory. Besides, Nubian women prefer to shop from the public *suq* (market), which moves from one place to another on specific days every week. This gives them an opportunity to get away from home and visit with relatives and friends in neighboring villages.

The Ministry of Supply also provided wheat flour and bread for the new settlements. A grain mill was set up in Nasr Town, and seventeen mechanized bakeries were established in a number of Nubian villages. Thirteen of the bakeries have closed down for lack of business because after the Nubians settled down in their new homes they stopped buying bread and went back to baking it at home as was their custom in Old Nubia. Baking bread at home is considered more economical. In addition, the traditional kinds of Nubian bread usually associated with certain rites and social situations are not available in the public bakeries.

The failure of these bakeries suggests that two main factors should be considered in terms of food supply. One is the nutritional factor, dealing with calories, protein, starch, etc., while the other emphasizes minimum requirements and other such constraints. This particular factor, although necessary, is not felt to be the most critical in studying resettlement. In planning relocations, providing basic nutritional needs is important, but the crucial issue is one regarding such things as taste and cost, especially where tradition is involved. Tradition notwithstanding, the slight variations in taste for very similar foods provides an outlet for expressing dissatisfaction that is perhaps caused by other factors. The influx of a community of people can cause a food shortage and a rise in the prices of various commodities; many Nubians traveled quite a distance to obtain fresh fruit and vegetables. The same tastes and likes will not exist for all such communities but fundamental traits do exist. Thus, in addition to the nutritional aspects, questions of tradition are important. As time goes on, preferred tastes and food may change as the people adapt to their new homeland.

PUBLIC SECURITY

The services of the Ministry of Interior in Old Nubia were confined to a single police station in Eneba, which was then the administrative center of the region. Village *omdas* (headmen) and *shaykhs* (religious leaders) were also entrusted with matters of security as the representatives of the authorities in the villages and hamlets. Official records indicate that security was well-established in Old Nubia, particularly if compared to the region of Upper Egypt (north of Nubia), where the incidence of crime is the highest in the country. (Only one case of homicide has been reported, in 1975, in New Nubia since its establishment.) There were naturally disputes between individuals and tribes over land or irrigation, but they were usually peacefully settled through traditional practices without resort to outside authority. Also, despite the great distances that set the villages apart, the homogeneity of the population and the kinship relations between individuals contributed greatly to the prevailing security.

The structure of the Kom Ombo settlement created a lack of homogeneity among the inhabitants of the Nubian villages and hamlets, which had either been amalgamated or built very close to one another, and Nubians found themselves close neighbors of non-Nubian groups. In addition, the very experience of resettlement brought with it a certain degree of maladjustment and psychological instability that may last for some time. In the light of these circumstances, the Ministry of Interior has been concerned about making security services widely available and has established a central police station in Nasr Town in addition to other police outposts in the principal villages. A fire-station unit has also been set up at Nasr Town.

EDUCATION AND VOCATIONAL TRAINING

The government actually contributed little to education and vocational training in Old Nubia. Its efforts were limited to setting up schools in Irmina and Dakka for teacher training, a secondary school in Eneba, and a number of primary schools in other villages. The difficulty of travelling from one village or hamlet to another forced many children to depend entirely for their education on the village *kuttab*, or Qur'an school, where boys and girls assembled in a single room to receive instruction in elementary reading and writing and to memorize the Qur'an at the hands of the village *shaykh*.

This situation has changed. The government has established nineteen primary schools (with 162 classes), distributed so that each school serves two or three neighboring villages within a radius of not more than three kilometers. Three preparatory schools with twenty-four classes have been established to provide vocational education and training in keeping with the agricultural and industrial conditions in New Nubia.

The settlers have participated in the establishment of three primary and three preparatory schools. In secondary education, New Nubia has a secondary school in Nasr Town, with six classes and boarding facilities for students coming from distant villages. The school is equipped with workshops and the material needed for vocational instruction.

SOCIAL WELFARE AND HEALTH SERVICES

Social services were not readily accessible to the remote Nubian hamlets prior to resettlement since there was only one social agency for each region. This agency was in charge of implementing social welfare services for needy cases. In Nubia today, there are six social agencies that take care of social welfare problems and four agencies combining the services of education, health, and social welfare. Through these agencies Nubian children have a UNICEF-sponsored program for vocational training, nursery care, cottage-craft education, and house management. As to youth services, there are thirty-five centers for sports, recreation, and educational activities. In two villages that lacked such facilities, Nubians took the initiative in raising local funds and getting donations from relatives working in cities in order to construct youth centers for their own people. The village youth centers' sport and social activities function effectively as an integration channel for the three ethnic groups, and they are a means of contact with the host community as well. The centers also managed to establish wide contacts with Nubian city associations not only for exchange visits and sport programs but also to get them to function as liaisons between urbanite Nubians and local residents of New Nubia. Consequently, these associations today are no longer centers for charity and entertainment as traditionally used to be the case; instead, they have become active units for handling Nubian problems with authorities in the capital.

Health services were planned and implemented to raise the health standard of the Nubian relocatees from what had been the traditional situation. The dispersion of small villages along the Nile in the old setting made it extremely difficult for many Nubians to have access to government medical care. There was only a twenty-bed hospital located in the central town of Eneba in addition to limited hospitalization service offered by a German missionary in the northern part of Old Nubia. In southern Nubia, health services, especially in connection with epidemic disease control, were provided to inhabitants by means of river steamer. In effect, government health services were very limited and of marginal use to Nubians, who depended mainly on their folkways in the diagnosis and treatment of diseases. Their folk medicine was tied to their belief system, local environment (especially for medicinal ingredients), and ceremonial practices.

The response of Nubians to government medical services has been exceptionally favorable. The relocatees believe that the provision of medical services is a positive consequence of resettlement. Health officials indicate that the positive response of the Nubians to improved medical services has probably contributed to the lowering of the crude death rate, especially among infants. Available statistics indicate a tendency toward a lower death rate after a rather unusual rise during the two years immediately following relocation. (Note the indications of stress in the relocation experience demonstrated by this peak in the death rate.) The crude death rate was 17 in 1974 in contrast to an average of 23 for the years 1964–65. Yet, it is still higher than a national rate of 14.5 per thousand for 1974 as well as a yearly average death rate of 14 per thousand between 1956 and 1959, prior to resettlement.

Records in 1972 show that a substantial number of Nubians visited out-patient clinics. There was also a waiting list for people applying for hospitalization. However, the scene of men, women, and children crowded into clinics should not, according to local doctors, imply the existence of an ailing community. Rather, it reflects a common desire among the relocatees to benefit as much as possible from the free medical services, whether or not they actually need them. On market days, for instance, including a visit to the health clinic has become routine practice, especially among those women who regularly shop at the weekly market. The doctors also point out that many clients do not mind waiting for hours just to complain of very minor things such as a "simple headache," or a "finger scratch," or to ask for vitamins for themselves and relatives. The feeling among the relocatees is, doctors assume, "Why not make use of a free service?" When asked why they go to the clinic for such minor matters, informants do express such an attitude.

Despite the improved medical services and the good use Nubians have made of them, their folk medicine continues to exist, although with some accommodations. For cases of cold and dysentery, for example, folk medicine is used in addition to doctors' prescriptions. If the ingredients for folk medicine are not available in the new habitat, doctors' prescriptions are followed. The general tendency, however, is to substitute "clinic medicine"—to use informants' terminology—for their traditional medicine only in case of organic diseases. But mental illness continues to have its folk practioners and treatment. "This is not the kind of illness that one takes to the clinic doctor. We have our specialized doctors"—to quote an informant. Diseases, in the Nubians' view, fall into two major categories: one related to the body, i.e., organic; the other connected to the mind, i.e., mental. Organic diseases can be cured by either folk or clinic medicine, but mental illness requires a complex set of ceremonial diagnoses and treatments, which come under the realm of traditional Nubian folk medicine rather than clinic treatment.

One medical service that received a minimum response from the relocatees has been the distribution of contraceptives. Like other rural areas in Egypt, New Nubia was provided with family-planning clinics where birth-control pills would be available free of charge. Records, however, indicate a very limited response and a high percentage of dropouts among registered clients. There are many reasons, technical and human, that cause such lack of interest. To cite a few examples, the pill seems to be an inappropriate contraceptive device given the irregular "at home" pattern of absent husbands. Moreover, Nubians would prefer to have a large population to cope with the dominant neighboring groups rather than a "shrinked community," as one local Nubian leader commented. Female modesty, a husband's rejection of the pill as a birth-control method, and discomfort from side effects were other reasons often reported by women for refusing to use the pill. Whatever the reasons may be, the significant question is whether Nubians actually need birth control.

Chapter Seven
Men, Women, and Resettlement Politics

The Nubian steadiness, patience, reliability, truthfulness, respon-
sibility, hospitality and neighbourly love would not easily find an
equivalent in the world. It is remarkable that these people knew
how to preserve these qualities all through the decades of increas-
ing difficulties.

Anna Hohenwart (1963:168)

Background

The patterns of interaction that begin to emerge in a resettlement
setting are basic to conceptualizing the dynamics of adaptation to
displacement and in determining its process and coping mechanism.
A close look at the Nubian setting at Kom Ombo identifies three
major groups or entities that influence present and future conditions
of the displaced community. The Nubian relocatees represent the
basic entity for a wider spectrum of interaction at different levels. The
setting is further complicated by the ethnic and linguistic dissimilarities
of the three displaced Nubian groups: the Kenuz, the Arabs, and the
Fedija. Prior to resettlement each of these groups occupied a well-
defined region and maintained their distinct ecological, social, and
linguistic features. Also, when the relocated community has city labor
migrants and residents as a part of its population, the involvement
and impact of that urban extension greatly influence the coping strategies to relocation.

In addition, and equally important, is the challenge of coping with
an unfamiliar environment, including the indigenous inhabitants,
often referred to as the host group. One significant variable in influ-

97

encing the nature and dynamics of these relationships has been the population growth of the three ethnic groups after relocation. Census data of 1960, 1966, and 1967 show that there had been variations in the growth of the population size of each ethnic group. This was mainly due to the volume of in- and out-migration. The Kenuz group, for instance, increased in number 24.8 percent between 1960 and 1966. But in November 1976, the Kenuz, who had numbered almost twenty-one thousand in 1966, showed a decrease to only 15,856. For the Arab group the demographic situation was different: Their number almost doubled by 1966 (from 4,418 in 1960 to 8,846 people in 1966). Nonetheless, by 1976 this figure had decreased to 6,284. Similarly the Fedija, who showed a slight increase during the period 1960–66, witnessed a considerable rate of population decrease (5.6 percent) over the period 1966–76.

The flow of Fedija people from urban areas to Old or New Nubia had been small compared to that of the Arab group, whose population doubled between 1960 and 1966. Prior to resettlement, the Fedija group was the largest (about 64 percent of the total population in 1960) and economically better off since their region was the least affected by the old dam and its subsequent heightenings. The Arab Nubians were largely deprived of cultivated lands; and the Kenuz land, the closest to the dam, was most affected. This difference in population increase among the three Nubian groups may suggest variations in the flow of people into and out of New Nubia rather than changes in the pattern of natural increase.

Assuming that the sex ratio would reflect an absentee phenomenon among the male population, the following figures may provide further evidence that the migration pattern largely determines the population dynamics in New Nubia. Among the Fedija, the sex ratio was 71 men to 100 women in 1960 and became 88:100 in 1966; it then reached 99:100 in 1976. The sex ratio among the Kenuz was 53:100 in 1960, increased to 59:100 in 1966, and decreased to 55:100 in 1976. For the Arab group, the sex ratio showed a remarkable increase from 50:100 in 1960 to 80:100 in 1966, and then a decrease to 62:100 in 1976. In Chapter Five it was pointed out that the migration pattern has no immediate correlation to the economic conditions among the three Nubian groups. Nevertheless, it seems evident that, unlike the rest of the country, population dynamics in New Nubia are not determined by the reproduction of more people but rather by the migration phenomenon among the relocatees.

RESETTLEMENT AND ETHNICITY

Upon relocation, the three ethnic groups found themselves in close physical proximity and engaging in intensive social interaction. The first step in the interaction process resulted when, shortly after relocation, they had to deal with their shared problems. This necessitated immediate contacts among the three groups, forcing them to unite in their demands to the administration. Consequently, a sense of identification with a common community was emphasized, thus enabling them to function as a sustaining force, not in terms of ethnic affiliation or attributes.

This new sense of unity coincided with the aspirations of the local Nubian leaders, creating an advantageous situation in which they could gain seats in the people's council. It also benefited the government, which could now deal with a unified community in terms of administration.

Although this was the case at the community level, traditional rivalry continued to exist, especially between the Kenuz and the Fedija, expressing itself in the competitive outlets of politics, sports, and community development projects. In the area of politics, for instance, a delicate balance was established; votes were cast in 1976 for two candidates, one from the Kenuz and the other from the Fedija, to represent the entire Nubian community in the People's National Council in Cairo. This delicate balance is maintained by having the Arab group, a minority within the Nubian community, function as a "swing" group. To make up for the differences in the size of population of each group and the proportion of absent males, each group encouraged its female enclave to register and vote.

The women's vote was then used as a political card not only in the hands of the three Nubian groups but also to outnumber the Saiydis and gain the balance of political power. This tactic led to the orientation of women to political affairs; and in the 1976 election, the women, out of twenty thousand registered Nubians, cast fourteen thousand votes. Women are allowed to vote according to the Egyptian electoral law, but it is still not permitted in many areas, especially in the conservative region of Kom Ombo. Such pressures caused the Nubians to operate through their socially valued norms, which will undoubtedly have a definite influence on the Aswan region not only politically but culturally as well.

In sports and other activities, including education, the competition and pride of each of the various groups is manifested in terms of raising money from Nubians in the cities in order to build and maintain youth clubs. In Qustul, a Fedija village, a youth club was built in 1970; and in Dahmit, a Kenuz village, money was collected to build a high school, thus saving its children the long daily commute to the only Nubian high school, located in Nasr Town. Both sexes are registered in the schools, a practice still uncommon in many areas, and this factor alone should have a powerful influence on the educational incentive among the Nubians.

Daily contacts in the Kom Ombo markets, government offices, schools, and political meetings are also factors directly affecting the interaction of the three groups. As long as a common language (Arabic) is spoken, communication is possible, although ethnic sensitivities and rivalries have continued to exist. Intermarriage is still quite limited (in 1975 informants reported only two cases), and interaction continues dependent on necessity and common interest, to use an informant's words.

Relations with the Hosts

The Saiydis, the host group, are more conservative than the Nubians. Physical characteristics also differ: The Nubians are tall and dark, and the Saiydis are shorter and have lighter skin. The stereotype of the Saiydis is that of conservatism and toughness. During the first few months following resettlement, Nubians formed youth patrols to prevent Saiydi peddlers from neighboring villages entering Nubian residential areas. At night, gunshots were often fired to warn intruders. Women used to walk in groups in the daytime, and, at night, they were permitted to go out only in the company of men.

This attitude did not last long, however. The need for the Saiydis' expertise in cultivating and harvesting the sugarcane compelled the Nubians to establish a rapport with the host group out of economic necessity. On the part of the Saiydis, they favored and encouraged this rapprochement on both economic and political grounds because they needed "Nubian money and votes," in the words of a Nubian village head. The Saiydis, who did not allow their women to vote, had to collaborate with the Nubians in order to maintain a balance of power for their own community. In 1976 the Nubians held 30 percent of the total registered vote for the entire Kom Ombo region.

The relationship between the two groups continued on the basis of this unwritten accord without extending to social matters. But as years went by, restrictions on interaction between the two groups began to ease off as the Nubians' fears were dispelled and interaction became necessary for coping with resettlement problems.

New Role for Nubian Associations

Resettlement enhanced contact between the Kom Ombo settlers and their fellowmen working and living in urban areas in Egypt and abroad. The location of the new settlement facilitated the contact between rural and urban enclaves of the Nubian community. It is now only one hour by plane from Cairo to Aswan (some forty kilometers away from Kom Ombo), while a direct night train takes approximately thirteen hours to reach Kom Ombo coming from Cairo. In the old days before resettlement, the trip would take an additional four to thirteen hours by boat, depending on the destination from Aswan. The post boat was the only link with the outside, and its arrival with mail and news was a community event as it sailed from shore to shore, passing by most villages.

This isolation has changed now, and the urban Nubian associations, particularly the two Nubian clubs in Cairo and Alexandria, have served as channels for organized contacts between the two enclaves. The clubs are no longer places of accommodation and entertainment; members now serve the Nubians by submitting and defending their demands and requests to the government headquarters in Cairo. These clubs organized conferences and workshops to discuss problems with government officials; and in February 1975 they began to publish a bimonthly journal called *Akhbar el-Nuba*, "News of Nubia." The clubs also function in providing substantial assistance through the professional experience of its members by soliciting donations from and making contacts with the Egyptian authorities to facilitate development projects such as schools and youth clubs. From 1977 on, these clubs also played a significant role in advocating and supporting the desire of Kom Ombo Nubians to return to their homeland (discussed in detail in the next chapter).

It is also interesting to note that as Nubians in Kom Ombo mobilized the women's vote to cope with the political struggle in the region and to maintain a balance of power to their benefit, Nubian women in Cairo were also recruited to play a political and social role in support of the Nubian cause within the context of national development. As a result, and for the first time in Nubian history, Nubian women of Cairo, most of them university graduates, formed an association in 1978. A year later the government granted the association a land lot on which to build a headquarters. In the same year the association began issuing its monthly magazine, *Ganoub el-Wadi*, "Southern Valley," for the purpose of education and to disseminate news about the Nubians, the Saiydis, and other groups living in Upper Egypt. Once again Nubians demonstrated that they do not consider themselves a distinct and isolated minority group, but rather part of a region (Upper Egypt) and a nation (Egypt).

In June 1980, the Minister of Social Affairs granted the Nubian women's association a certificate of appreciation for its role in social welfare in the community and for serving the state's development goals by teaching Nubian girls and women handicrafts and advising them about national development themes. Members of the association also organized and made trips to the lake region to stimulate interest in the move back to the homeland. The groups included women of all ages, family members, and children; and it was hoped that women would prove to be influential with the men in their families in promoting the move back. By 1980 the women's association had extended its activities to other Egyptian cities and had also established a link with Nubian associations abroad.

In an earlier report on how Nubians responded to resettlement during the first two years (Fahim 1968), I indicated that resettlement had provided women with opportunities that could result in drastic changes in their lives and roles in the society. Prior to resettlement, Nubian women enjoyed much more freedom of movement and assumed a major role in running most family affairs in a community whose men were absent most of the time. The resettlement created a sudden vacuum in the lives of women. In Old Nubia, the daily round of work completely absorbed their energies, while in the new communities women had many hours of unaccustomed leisure (Fernea and Kennedy 1966:352). Also, men became overprotective, thus limiting much of the women's former activities. But women, while confined to their villages, began working on remodeling the government houses to resemble their old homes.

As reported by Fernea and Kennedy, "Nubian women have supplemented and diversified the family diet by buying chicks, lambs, and kids to replace mature livestock lost in transit. The scarcity of animal food was at first a deterrent to such activities, but some women searched great distances for grass, and some villagers rented land from Saiydi farmers to grow fodder. Within a few months, most homes had at least one milk goat, and keeping livestock has gradually become more feasible as more Nubian families receive cultivable land from the government. Furthermore, many women quickly developed small vegetable gardens in their courtyards, irrigating them with water from the public taps despite official efforts to discourage this use of relatively scarce potable water. These plots resemble the small gardens made in Old Nubia by carrying alluvial soils up onto the sand" (1966:204).

Women responded positively and made good use of health services. Moreover, and interestingly enough, their election votes helped the Nubian community assume invaluable weight in regional politics. A corollary to this new political role of women is the growing interest in educating girls. Unlike other groups in this conservative area of Kom Ombo, Nubians have a permissive attitude regarding education for girls and only a few years after relocation began to encourage women to hold government jobs. These developments and emerging attitudes regarding the role of women in the New Nubian community will probably accelerate sociocultural change. However, Nubian women's role in change is not restricted to serving as tools manipulated by other forces, for they also take the initiative and help men in dealing with resettlement problems, working together to shape the future of their community.

THE NUBIANS AND THE ADMINISTRATION

The collaboration between the urban and rural Nubian groups evolved into a close encounter with local relocation authorities and policy-makers at the government level, who have the real power,

according to an informant, "to induce change if it is so desired."
At the local level the immediate result of the interaction between the
Nubians and the relocation administrators was a confrontation. The
administrators were surprised and displeased to find the Nubians
ungrateful, believing the government "owed them something" for
forcing them to leave their homeland. Traditional suspicions and the
poor conditions found in the area increased the negative feelings of
the Nubians toward the relocation authorities.

Consequently, the Nubians exercised what I consider "tactful
pressure" in the form of petitions and complaints in dealing with the
relocation-related problems. An individual would draft a complaint or
submit a petition to the local officials along with copies to their superi-
ors, including the governor of the Aswan region. The complaints soon
multiplied, becoming too numerous to handle, especially during the
two years following relocation; and when the Nubians received negative responses they then submitted the complaints to top officials in
Cairo, who in turn transferred them back to the local authorities.
Realizing their problems were common to many, the Nubians found
it more effective to approach the authorities in organized groups.

Representatives from these groups formed delegations to present
the complaints, and it gradually became a matter of daily routine for
Nubians to meet with public officials to discuss their problems. It was
not at all unusual to see Nubians going from house to house, getting
signatures on complaints and collecting contributions for paperwork
and travel expenses. This approach caught the attention of the
administrators, who were impressed by the organized and tactful
manner of the unprecedented protest campaign. One top official,
commenting on the immense volume of grievances flooding his office,
exclaimed, "Many Nubians seem to be obsessed by writing complaints."

These complaints were combined with subtle pressure tactics by
the many Nubians who worked in the presidential quarters, the
homes of ministers, and in private clubs, and who thus had access to
people in power. These political tactics and the interaction between
Nubians and officials resulted in the formation of differing attitudes
and opinions among the Nubians toward each administrative division,
such as agriculture, health, housing, and social welfare, based on the
benefits received, in medical services for example, and the problems
encountered, especially with the agricultural administration.

The differing cultural attitudes and life-styles of the administrators and the settlers also made sympathetic communication difficult, and this added to the contradictory feelings between them. As Fernea points out, "Administrators, frequently coming from the cities are inevitably better educated than the settlers, are sometimes frustrated by the conditions of life on the resettlement projects as they lack amenities they are accustomed to, and they miss the pattern of associations they left behind in the city. Their personal unhappiness may make them apathetic to the settlers' needs, and they are thus not inclined to become involved in the local community in a way which would make them aware of the settlers' needs and desires" (1979:28).

It is interesting to note that Nubians approached resettlement problems with defense mechanisms, such as protecting their cultural traditions and customs, by extending relationships to the host community with caution and reserve and also by adopting the policy of "Nubianizing their community" through recruitment of educated Nubian youths to fill administrative positions and jobs created by the construction and industrial activities in the region. This project continues, directed toward all Nubians regardless of their ethnic background, and is designed to fill the community needs in specialized fields such as education, medicine, and agriculture.

The result of these efforts has been an increased political participation by Nubians that extends beyond regional affairs. This is a reflection of their unique ability to mobilize and fill key positions in the hierarchy of the Arab Socialist Union, the only functioning political organization in the country until 1976, when other parties were formed. Their urban experience and education enabled them to occupy leading posts in most government departments.

Thus, their cultural values have led to the Nubians' becoming a determining factor in the socioeconomic development of the area, filling the growing demand for special clerical skills and services, and playing a major part in the political and administrative roles in the governorate of Aswan. This unusual achievement for a group who had been isolated for so long seems to be the direct result of two factors. The first factor involves the freedom of choice that arose from their cultural pattern of migration, which seems to be a direct influence of the Nubians' ability to act and integrate themselves into the previously established community.

The second factor in this rapid development is a direct result of the Nubian resettlement in such a compact area. The government policies were developed with the idea of keeping the Nubian community intact by resettling the people on a site with well-defined boundaries rather than in dispersed communities with non-Nubian groups. This has resulted in keeping the culture intact, but it also gave the Nubians no alternative for expansion except outward into the larger community.

The Nubians were in a precarious situation, and if they had remained in a community that did not allow for growth, they would perhaps have turned inward and eventually regressed since the opportunities for advancement were relatively limited. To their credit they have continued to combine their strengths to such a degree that they have not only met the challenge of relocation, but have risen above it, expanding in the cultural direction that best suits them as Nubians. Whether they will eventually adapt as resident farmers in the years ahead seems questionable. Nonetheless, they have chosen alternatives supported by their traditions and culture.

PART III
RECENT DEVELOPMENTS AND FUTURE TRENDS

Past events that occurred between 1963 and 1977 and recent developments in the years between 1977 and 1980 may argue for the point of view that the transitional period lasted just two or three years after relocation. That the Nubians quickly took the initiative and began independently to cope with socioeconomic problems related to relocation may further the argument. But how can the transitional period be considered over while the Nubians have not yet adjusted and, as of 1980, were returning, although in limited numbers, to their original homeland and at the same time expanding the scale of their traditional pattern of labor migration? This suggests the necessity for further thinking about the process and length of the transition period. It also establishes the need for a set of technical and human indicators that would assess progress toward adaptation to new settings and determine the eventual termination of transition.

While the beginning of a transitional period may be easily identified at a specific time (when relocation plans become known), its termination depends upon the functioning of several factors and variables which, if identified and accounted for in the planning, will result in a much shorter transition period than if they are neglected or underestimated. Nonetheless, adjustment to one aspect or component of relocation may be a terminating point of transition in that particular setting, while the transitional period may go on and on for other aspects or components of adjustment. Resettlement often results in psychological problems, some of which may disappear as the relocatees achieve progress toward adjustment. Others may endure, thereby hampering the adjustment process.

   The Nubian relocatees, for instance, felt grief for losing a beloved homeland; they also worried a great deal due to uncertainty about life in the new location. Moreover, they felt disappointed because of unfulfilled government promises when they found themselves, from the very moment of resettlement, dependent on the government for food and shelter. Such characteristics of grief, worry, disappointment, fear, and dependency, which may occur in all resettlement situations in varying degrees, should be kept to a minimum and effectively tackled. Otherwise, they can easily result in an increasingly negative attitude toward adjustment and, especially for adults and the elderly, can delay indefinitely the feeling of being at home. As Scudder and Colson put it, "For some, specially the elderly, the transitional stage ends only with death. On the other hand, the transition stage rarely lasts longer than a generation since children who are born and brought up in the new habitat tend to feel at home there" (1982:280).

   I have found Smelser's concepts of "differential vulnerability to stress" and "differential availability of responses" helpful in understanding the situation in New Nubia (1968). Prior to relocation, life in Nubia had not been totally stress-free, especially in terms of limited economic resources and the social cost incurred by labor migration and particularly among the Kenuz and Arab groups. Nubians, however, had developed adequate coping mechanisms to deal with both environmental and social problems. In New Nubia, the situation is quite different regarding the types of stress, its intensity and implications. Some of the traditional coping strategies worked for certain problems but others proved to be ineffective, thus forcing the Nubians to search for alternatives or a totally new outlet.

   In this vein, Trimble, drawing upon his cross-cultural analysis of coping strategies to forced migration, has found that, "while living in their ancestral lands, the Kreen-Akrore and Bikinians had maintained well-established patterns of responding to stress situations. These patterns were deeply ingrained, and to an extent overlearned. The patterns were also an integral part of the folk history and folk psychiatry of the culture. In fact, the patterns were very much a part of their total ecological perspective. Sudden change, brought on by forced migration, exposed individuals to new environments. Under these conditions, traditional responses for dealing with stress became ineffective for dealing with the realities that follow migration (Reusch,

Jacobson, and Loeb 1948). On the surface, it would appear that the relocation experiences of the four groups described earlier introduced new forms of stress. Traditional forms of responding to the stress appeared to be ineffective; if they had been effective, the communities would be in far better position than they are today. Westermeyer (1978:121) suggests that 'some aspects of culture might be more ecology sensitive while others are nonecology resistant.' It may be that stress reactions are least resistant especially among cultural groups with fairly rigid ways of responding to stressful situations" (Trimble 1980:470).

As indicated earlier, community relocation is a multifaceted process of a difficult task; its understanding requires, therefore, a multidisciplinary perspective and a careful identification and assessment of all factors and variables involved. Resettlement may be viewed and analyzed and evaluated with a variety of paradigms, including economics, psychological and sociocultural approaches or models; yet, I feel that resettlement results in a serious crisis in a community's general health, mainly in terms of mental illness and its effects on adaptation in the new setting. In "Community health aspects of Nubian resettlement in Egypt," I viewed these aspects as an especially useful index for assessing the dynamics of adaptation and rehabilitation among the displaced Nubians (1979a).

Chapter Eight elaborates on this point in the context of current tendencies by several Nubian groups to return home, i.e., to reestablish a Nubian life-style on the lake's shores. It also examines the return to a beloved land in terms of a proposed concept, namely "resettlement illness," which distinguishes between diseases that relocation actually brought about—or those that Nubians already had before resettlement —and the state of "feeling ill" as a result of resettlement. The underlying assumption here is that if the impact of uprooting on people is viewed as including not only the socioeconomic, but also the psychological and mental health aspects of the culture, then planners can structure policy propositions that will stimulate the positive aspects and prevent the inevitable stress through advanced, careful planning and an effective execution of the plan in fulfillment of the relocated society's needs.

Change seems to be inevitable for the Nubians; it was clearly going on in 1980, as it will in the future. If asked about the future, the

Nubians tend to be ambitious, yet pragmatic, for they realize their potential and are realistic concerning their limitations. Interestingly enough, they view the limitations to their ambitions in two ways: those that can be overcome by freedom of action, using their own abilities to confront conflicts and determine the direction they will choose, and others that are in the realm of the unforeseen, which they leave to the "care and blessing of God."

Nubians are Moslems and believe the fate of man is determined by his action and the "will of God." This attitude is not fatalistic, as many Western analysts have conceived it to be. For the Nubians it is a realistic approach to the problems of life in a place of limited resources and options for self-improvement and an effective coping mechanism in situations of crisis. It is within this framework that the Nubians approach the future by acting to mobilize their capabilities and resources and by depending on the "blessing of God."

These cultural attitudes must be considered a striking factor in the Nubians' return to their native land, for they have obviously been a determining factor in the development of their human resources. Their attitudes are especially relevant to their recent economic development, particularly the utilization of their own capital that continues to flow from the Nubian clubs in Cairo and Alexandria and from Nubian labor abroad, primarily from the Nubians working and living in London.

Chapter Nine reports on a group of Nubian migrants who have made a living far away from home—in London. This chapter is based upon information obtained during two visits with Nubians in London, which I made with Katherine Helmer in March 1978 and later in September 1978. Since 1979 I have visited the Nubians in London briefly on several occasions as my travelling schedule permitted.

Chapter Nine is a revised version of a report that Helmer wrote on the basis of our joint exploratory research and discussions (Helmer 1979). She authored this chapter except for the analytical commentary I offer at the end of it. The material in this chapter provides a case study of Nubians abroad. It focuses on their ties with families back home, their work, remittances, and how these may affect life in New Nubia or determine future trends. Given the increasing numbers of Nubians working outside Egypt, international migration is becoming an important coping strategy that Nubians have developed in response to economic hardship in New Nubia and the country as a whole. It is important, however, to realize that this international dimension in the migratory patterns among the Nubians, especially the youth, should not be attributed solely to resettlement. It is therefore essential in resettlement studies to distinguish between changes caused by relocation, and those that come about through external factors or as a result of the natural development of a society.

Chapter Eight
The Return to a Beloved Land

The Land of Nubia drowned in silence without crying or shedding tears. It now lies under water in Winter and Summer, too. . . . Alas, my land, my country and my Nubia. . . . My life had been there but my mother's grave and those of my ancestors now lie there. . . . In Nubia I also had my laughs and sighs; my days and dreams. But Nubia with its land, palm trees and my childhood has now settled down under water with dignity and pride. . . . O Nubia, you are the only true life.

By a Nubian poet and writer, Mohamed El Shourbagy, 1980 (translated from Arabic by HMF)

MOTHER NUBIA

A cultural environment is composed of a variety of images that create an atmosphere or space that affects the consciousness of the people. In the Nubian case, their surroundings created a rhythm, or cycle that was interwoven with their love for the aesthetic qualities of the land. Nubia was considered the "mother," and perhaps the enduring quality of the land and the Nile was an important factor affecting the patterns of labor migration, allowing them an inner feeling of independence and security even when far from home. The change in the physical environment directly affected the Nubian state of mind for it necessarily required an instinctive adaptation of roles and a resulting change in their nature.

Perhaps the most important cause underlying the Nubians' grief in the new community has been the absence of the Nile, which is taken as the "River of Life, the Divine Life" in the words of Nubian informants. It had been an integral part of their life and customs, and was often referred to by the Nubians as a "source of relief and creativity," connecting them with the rhythm of life itself. Consequently, Nile ceremonies in New Nubia have been entirely eliminated; the Nile is no longer there, and without it, in an informant's words, "Nubia is gone." For centuries the Nubians have been constantly in tune with the Nile's flow; and this was manifested in their cultural and spiritual ceremonies. Now, deprived of this beauty and life-giving qualities, the Nubians responded with a depression which goes far deeper than that related to the loss of a homeland and which has affected their attitude toward the quality of life in the new land. It is symbolically significant that the Nubians attributed their health problems to chemically treated potable water while referring to the Nile's water as "pure and blessed."

In 1975, nearly more than a decade following relocation, I was struck by the fact that the displaced Nubians had not yet overcome the resettlement aftermaths and had not yet psychologically settled in Kom Ombo. There was still evidence of what I had described in one of my earlier papers (1979a) as "resettlement illness," a concept that distinguishes between diseases that resettlement actually brought about—or those that Nubians already had before resettlement—and the state of "feeling ill" as a result of displacement. It is not my intention here to list the kind of diseases emerging from resettlement, as no empirical material is yet available, but it is widely assumed among officials that, for instance, the extension of irrigation in the relocation area and the increasing contact between men and water has resulted, or will result, in the spread of bilharzia (schistosomiasis). However, no before and after resettlement statistics are available to validate such an assumption. Doctors report finding cases of bilharzia among the relocatees, but they do not view the disease as widespread. It seems possible to predict limited incidences of bilharzia among the relocatees in contrast to the neighboring groups, since only 60 percent of the relocated Nubian families are landholders, of whom a large proportion are not actually doing the agricultural work themselves. Also, since children are encouraged to go to school, they are rarely seen doing agricultural work. Yet, children are exposed to the disease much more than men because of their frequent swimming and bathing in canals, especially on warm days.

When asked what new diseases had appeared and what old diseases had disappeared since resettlement, informants, mostly in the age range of thirty and above, responded that despite improved medical care, they were much healthier in their homeland. They "have become sick only in Kom Ombo." Old Nubia is "health," while New Nubia is "illness," an informant said. No old diseases have gone away; on the contrary, informants generally said, they have increased. Their list of new diseases included heart attacks, diabetes, high blood pressure, and mental disorder, to mention only the most common. Some informants mentioned crime, such as theft, mugging, and rape, as a serious new community disease brought about by resettlement. This runs contrary to the feeling of security they enjoyed in their old home villages, referred to as "the land of security and peace." While police records indicate a minimum crime incidence compared to the unusually high crime rate of the neighboring communities, police officials said that Nubian young men seem to have gradually copied some delinquent behavior from neighboring groups. Nevertheless, because of the common stereotypes of Nubians as honest and peaceful and of neighboring groups as aggressive and dishonest, the latter have always been scapegoats for whatever crime or delinquency occurs.

Among the things women complained of was physical fatigue. Some women informants indicated, more specifically, that in many cases giving birth is not as smooth as it used to be. In a similar vein, Fawzia Hussein, an Egyptian woman physical anthropologist who conducted research on the impact of resettlement on women's lives, explained to me that the limited physical movement of relocated women in contrast to what they were used to, combined with a long period of stressful life, possibly has affected their health conditions and in some cases their physiological performance. During the two years following resettlement, women were actually engaged in hard physical work such as gardening for food and assisting in remodeling their houses into better living quarters. Subsequently, their activities have become limited and take place mostly indoors or within the village boundaries.

Relocation affected not only the women's physical health but also their mental state. Female informants reported an increase in the incidence of psychological depression and mental disorder among Nubian women. Some reasons are related to the lack of privacy in crowded living quarters and the absence of the security they had previously in their old habitat. Georg Gerster was right, in my view, to believe that "the old architecture of the Nubian house aims to ease the mind of the departing husband" (1963:611). The new houses hardly provide such relief. While it was assumed that moving to the new land would provide better economic opportunities so men could turn into permanent village residents, it did not happen to the extent expected. Consequently, women found their men—whether husband, brother, son or father—once again absent and leaving them behind in a different setting in which women could not feel as safe or secure as they did in Old Nubia. In addition, women's responsibilities became much greater than before. They continued to be the guardian of traditions, in addition to the heavy burden of coping with the every-day household-related problems and challenges aggravated by a bad economic situation and inadequate housing.

Most people who complained of the state of individual and com-munity illnesses are in their late thirties and older. These "diseases" do exist, as doctors report, but are not widespread. Nubians may have had them before, but due to the lack of modern medical services they were probably unaware of them. Doctors informed me that Nubians often come to the clinic complaining of being ill and diagnosing their illness as high blood pressure or diabetes, while tests prove negative. This phenomenon suggests that Nubians subconsciously feel or imag-ine being ill to convince themselves and others that "New Nubia is particularly bad" and "relocation has actually been a misfortune." This attitude of rejecting the new situation seems to have contributed to the development of a "state of depression" among many Nubians, especially the elderly. During my visit of January 1975, I found that many Nubian informants talked frequently about the "good old days," tended to reject their present situation, and hope for very little in the future. In February 1975, when the government announced plans for settlement and development of the dam's lake, the desire to return to the original homeland was expressed. Although there were then opposing views, the fact remains that, if after a decade or more since resettlement, families are wanting to move out, this indicates examples of unsuccessful adaptation in the new environment. As a result, I pro-posed a community-health index to assess adaptation to relocation, not in terms of the availability and use of new medical services, but rather in terms of health in general as a state of being sound in body and mind. Relocatees may be in a better physical condition due to improved medical care and food aid; yet, unless their state of mind is also healthy, they are most likely to feel as "strangers in a foreign land" or "temporary settlers"—to use two informants' phrases—and consequently continue to be dissident and dependent.

In a 1977 article (for the newspaper *Nubia News*) entitled "The Return," Khalil Shefa, a Nubian writer, perceives the return to the lake's shores on the old site of Nubia as a "logistic move and an inevitable development." He describes Old Nubia as a "genuine environment" in contrast to New Nubia which he views as "false"; the former is "natural" while the latter is "artificial." He states "that is why Nubians since relocation have not felt [at] home in the new setting, and still do not feel secure nor settled. Neither the site, nor the scenery or the farming land could be compared to what Nubia previously had." Shefa also says that "Nubians have done their utmost in coping with the relocation crisis but in vain; existing living condition in Kom Ombo are not likely to improve, and the state of people's health continues to deteriorate. . . . The only hope left is to return to the mother land," he tells his fellow Nubians. "Returning to Old Nubia should become the reality, because living in New Nubia in the hope that things might get better is no more than a mirage." In an interview with Shefa in 1978, he told me that "the return to their beloved land then became an indisputable matter among all Nubians."

The government's assumption that time would heal, that it would only be a matter of one or two generations before Old Nubia was history, may not happen. My assessment of the situation in 1977 indicates that, after nearly fourteen years since relocation in 1963, most Nubians were still filled with a sense of belonging to their homeland, and expressed a desire to return. Nonetheless, while this desire to return reflects a troubled state of mind and indicates difficulties among the Nubians to feel at home in Kom Ombo, I view, contrary to a common belief in government circles, the return to the lake not as a mere "sentimental move" by "elderly people" but as a new political and economic coping strategy that would allow the Nubians to break out of confinement in the Kom Ombo area, where economic options and opportunities for growth and progress have reached their optimum. In addition to labor migrations, Nubians (as of 1980) were seeking other economic and cultural alternatives which they hope to explore on the lake's shores. "Resettlement illness" and the return to the beloved land are actually the outcome of the limited resources of New Nubia.

LAKE DEVELOPMENT POTENTIALITIES

The Egyptian government had established the Aswan Regional Planning Authority to enhance the economic and social development in the Aswan region following the construction of the dam. Emphasis was originally given to industry, agriculture, and human resources, but eventually attention was directed to the provision of research and planning for the lake's development. The United Nations Development Program (UNDP) responded positively to a government request for technical and financial assistance; and the Food and Agriculture Organization (FAO), acting as the executing agency for the UNDP, presented in 1975 a report to the Egyptian government that included the research findings on and development of recommendations for the lake. The UNDP/FAO government report indicated excellent prospects for the fishing industry, pointing out that the existing yield could be doubled, reaching some twenty-four tons per year. The agricultural potentialities were also impressive in terms of the large expanse of arable land and the variety of crops that could be cultivated. The uplands, areas above the 182-meter elevation, could be used to produce perennial horticultural crops with lift irrigation. In addition, about two hundred feddans, lying between the lake's periphery and the expected 182-meter elevation, could be cultivated by using subsoil moisture, with or without supplementary irrigation, depending on the crop growth, the shore's slope, and the distance from the lake.

The projected studies described the possibilities of a settlement for fishermen, most of whom have prior agricultural experience, which would result in a mixed economy. The establishment of a settlement of fishermen would stimulate community and public services. The fishermen, estimated to number around five thousand in 1975, live on their boats (except for short visits to their home villages in Upper Egypt). They are mostly Saidyis; the Nubians have not traditionally been fishermen. It is of interest to note that the lake fish have become taboo among some Nubians who feel the fish feed on their ancestors' remains.

In view of the lake resources, the Nubians expressed interest in lake development and felt it would relieve some overcrowding at Kom Ombo and ease the economic hardships particularly since they could take advantage of the recreation facilities and the possibilities for tourism. The dismantling of the famous Abu Simbel Temple and its reconstruction high above the 182-meter water level established this 5000 B.C. antiquity as a tourist attraction; and at the town of Abu Simbel, a small airport was constructed to receive tourists. A hydrofoil also links Aswan and Abu Simbel, which will encourage travel between the two areas.

NUBIANS AND THE RETURN

Following the government's announcement to develop the lake region according to the UNDP/FAO plans, the news began to spread, and the Nubians responded immediately by requesting that a government authority investigate the possibility of their returning to the lake's region; the Nubians justified their request on the basis of promises made earlier by the relocation authorities. Their request was also supplemented by a series of complaints regarding the deteriorating living conditions in the Kom Ombo settlement. At the official level, their petitions were received with understanding and sympathy, but it was soon evident that the government was not ready to consider a Nubian exodus to the lake's shores.

Consequently, the Nubians changed their tactics and began to take the initiative and advocate their willingness to take part in the implementation of the lake-development plans. They suggested, as a means of achieving these goals, the formation of a Nubian-funded and -managed agricultural cooperative to cultivate and settle the lands on the lake's shores. As this idea gained momentum and emotional support among the Nubians, advocates of the return increased in number and organized a vigorous campaign to dramatize their demands to return.

Two elderly Nubians, Awad Kirbash from the Kenuz, and Bashir Dawoud of the Fedija, assumed the responsibility for publicizing the idea of a proposed cooperative society and presenting it to the official circles. With the help of their associates, these two men sought endorsement from their fellow Nubians through contacts with the Nubian associations in Cairo and Alexandria. They were met with reserved and skeptical opinions, voiced by many Nubians who felt that such a move would be doomed to failure without government aid and wide support by the Nubian public. It was also suggested that before taking any serious action or making plans from a distance, a fact-finding mission should be sent to the lake region. Subsequently, the government responded positively to a Nubian request to sail down the lake for inspection; and on May 20, 1976, a Nubian delegation, headed by Awad and Bashir began a seven-day tour of the region to choose an adequate site and acquire a feeling for the lake conditions at that time and for future plans. These two men, accompanied by recruited specialists on soil and agriculture, studied the area intensely and eventually chose Abu Simbel as the most appropriate site. Their choice was based on several considerations. The government experimental agriculture station at Abu Simbel had an excellent yield from a variety of crops, including vegetables and fruits; the development of Abu Simbel as a tourist attraction would increase the potential job opportunities for Nubians; and the airport and roads that were scheduled for construction would completely eliminate the dreaded isolation. Meanwhile, the Sudanese government had already implemented several development plans for the Wadi Halfa region, which had become the closest habitable area to the Abu Simbel site. Nubians realized they could benefit from these plans, and also revive the Sudanese ties for the purpose of trade and commercial development that had been established prior to relocation. The Nubians also felt more secure at Abu Simbel due to its location at a relatively higher ground level, thus protected from fluctuations of the water level of the lake.

In view of the positive outcome of the May mission and in order to alleviate the reservations and opposition of certain Nubian groups, the formation of a multipurpose cooperative society was proposed to take care of farming the land and other economic activities.

Several months later the request for the formation of the society was granted, and its legal operation was announced in July 1977. During this period the Nubians engaged in an intensive, highly organized, multidimensional campaign to obtain government approval for their request. This group, led by the supporting advocates, obtained the backing of Osman Ahmed Osman, an eminent figure in the government, former minister of housing and reconstruction, and a close friend of President Sadat. Nubians requested that he become the

"Honorable Chairman of a Government Committee for the Reconstruction of Nubia," whose function was to serve as a liaison between them and the government departments involved in implementing the development plans.

"The Sadat Agricultural Cooperative Society" was officially proclaimed and licensed to operate. Following the formation of its board, a Nubian delegation headed by Awad, met with the president, and at their request a government committee for the reconstruction of Old Nubia was established. Three Nubian villages were proposed for construction, but the government maintained its commitment to merely provide for land reclamation, infrastructure, and the basic necessities such as water and a limited amount of equipment.

Although official recognition of the established Nubian enterprise in the Abu Simbel region was viewed as an accomplishment, Bashir revealed his feelings regarding the steps ahead. "We felt as though we were just stepping onto a long and difficult road, but we were thrilled. We can now count on the fellows and young men to pursue our goal of returning to the beloved land if we fail to live until this happens." This statement reflected not only his feelings, but the overwhelming enthusiasm of the Nubians in accepting the challenge of another resettlement, which will necessarily require continued struggle and dedication.

Bashir, Awad, and their supporters soon initiated a campaign to raise funds and solicit greater participation for the ambitious project. Response was favorable, and in October 1977 the Nubian Club met in Cairo to discuss its role in implementing the project. On November 10th I attended the club's meeting with the Nubian representatives in Alexandria, where the issue of return was the main topic. There was a tremendous response from the Nubian associations to the request to send representatives, especially young men who attended many of the meetings concerning the project. Their enthusiasm was unusual, for many of them had never seen Old Nubia but were familiar only with its history and culture through their families.

Recognizing the value of political support, the Nubians tied their campaign to the political and economic rapprochement between the Sudan and Egypt. In October 1977, the Egyptian and Sudanese parliaments met to discuss the economic and cultural integration of the two countries. Among the proposals presented was a joint project for the development of the lake shores behind the dam. Responding to the Egyptian/Sudanese alliance, members of the Nubian Club acted immediately by organizing a rally that marched through the streets of Cairo to symbolize their concern and support for the proposed integration as well as to advocate an important role for them to play in its realization and success.

The Nubian leadership viewed these joint meetings as an excellent opportunity to promote interest among Nubians for their return to the homeland. Realizing the value of their close kinship ties with the Sudanese Nubians, they publicized their potential role for achieving a cultural and economic linkage between the two countries. If resettled in Abu Simbel, only seventy kilometers from the Sudanese border, the relationships would not only benefit the Nubians but the two nations as well. Sensing the political potential of the situation, Nubian leaders held several sessions with members of the Sudanese parliament while visiting in Cairo, expressing their views on the present and the future of the Nubian community in Egypt and presenting their proposed plans to settle on the lake's shores.

NUBIANS FACE THE CHALLENGE

Being aware of existing difficulties in the Kom Ombo settlement, the government supported the return of the Nubians to the lake's shores, but on their initiative. In other words, the government did not commit itself to a direct involvement in any sponsored Nubian exodus from Kom Ombo. The Nubians, however, requested the authorities to provide the necessary physical infrastructure that would allow the returnees to make a living along the lake's shores. The Nubians also found the nationwide criticism of the side effects of the dam an opportunity to present their cause and grievances to public opinion, and they did succeed in gaining a lot of sympathy, so much so that a Nubian delegation met with President Sadat in 1978. The meeting with the president was inspiring, especially to Awad who commented, "Who would believe that five ministers have been instructed by the President to help the Nubians establish new villages on the lake's shores." But time passed by, and the Nubians were left struggling alone. Arguments ensued with the government concerning the problems of transportation, construction, and costs, and as a result hope of resettlement slowly began to fade, at least for a while.

At this point fifty men from two of the Fedija villages, Adendan and Qustul, decided to take pioneering action. Gathering a few essentials for living on the desert, these Nubians, aged 25 to 50 and of diverse backgrounds, made plans to sail down the lake to the site of their old villages. The following is an extract from a translation from Arabic of an interview with one of the men by Mohamed Omer Bakheit of *Nub*, a publication of the Society for Revival of Nubian Heritage.

> Well, the first steps were of course to organize ourselves; people of our village [Adendan] in Kom Ombo [disagreed with] us. They said to those of us who wanted to return that we were crazy, . . . that it was dangerous, and [that] the government would not let us. But we were determined to die if necessary in our trip to our old ground.
>
> We went to the [governor of Aswan], but he was hesitant; also the government [opposed] us. We disagreed with Awad Kirbash's idea; we did not want to live just anywhere surrounded by anyone; we wanted Nubia like it was with the same family, [the] same neighbours. God in his benevolence gave us the miracle of our land back, after we thought we would be landless for eternity. Anyway, although Kirbash's organization had the financial backing and knew more government people, we decided not to wait for them [but to] start out all alone by ourselves. We were lucky because under the great President Sadat's program of "Developing New Communities" any community can obtain permission to make [empty land fertile and green].
>
> It was my idea that we register with the Ministry of Agriculture, so that we might have help and [have our cause] be legitimate. You know we [people of Adendan and those of Qustul] said, "Really we need no one's help; we will succeed on our own." Also we said, "Each region should register in its own area and obtain their own facilities. The government is poor and we should not worry them." The people in our villages who objected were . . . used to cities and modernity, and also . . . some women [had become] lazy here with water in pipes, ovens, television, and [the ease of] shopping in Kom Ombo and Aswan. But really that was not many; everybody longed to return, but only a few were willing to work for it. You know it was the old men who were most willing to leave. Anyway, we raised money in our village by selling anything we could.
>
> Our brothers in Cairo contacted a great, great man [who is the owner of a Sudanese-Egyptian shipping line.] We said to him, "We want to rent one of your steamers to take us and our belongings to Abu Simbel. How much do you want?" He said, "For free of course." He is a real Nubian.

. . . .

On October 16, 1978, thirty-seven people from [Adendan and Qustul] took off by steamer headed for Abu Simbel. If you knew what was about to happen to us you would [want to] make it into an adventure film. Our first difficulty was that we were delayed . . . , and a great squabble broke out on whether to return or not. Most of us, of course, said, "No way, [we will] never go back to ridicule and that Kom Ombo misery." Anyway, God willed it and we sailed away.

After an exhausting trip we arrived at Abu Simbel. It was heaven; I cannot describe it; we were all revived. The air was so fresh, some of us cried; but also we realized that this mass of water covered whole villages and our grandparents' graves.

That day and night we slept there and we were greeted by our Nubian brothers in Abu Simbel. Believe me they were as overjoyed as we were that across the shore life would begin again. Our group was mostly older people, but we had planned a good group [who were] hard working, experienced in farming, planning villages, and nursing.

.   .   .   .

After 4 days of preparation in Abu Simbel, representatives from the Wadi Kom Ombo Construction company (sent by the Ministry of Reconstruction, responsible for new communities) and the Rigwa soil-testing company arrived to cross over with us.

The boat docked in a cove, and we set up tents and wooden shacks in the potential locations. That . . . first morning while scouting around we saw hyenas and cobras, so our very first task was to exterminate these within our habitable areas. Thanks be to God, there was little sandstone in the chosen location, which meant fertile soil. In the next few harsh weeks the Kom Ombo company set up some scaffolding for irrigation, but all the manual work was done by us.

These people had left their families behind and, as Awad Kirbash told me, "there was a unique spiritual drive about their actions as they worked day and night." Their sustaining slogan, "our bodies may be tired but our souls are relieved," helped them to endure their isolation. A new point of view emerged from this situation, and is indicated by the name they chose to give to their village. They named it "Integration." Until that time it had been a mere concept, but now, coinciding with the government's political venture for integration, it became reality.

At the beginning of relocation, the Nubians had clung to the old names of their villages, asking the government to name the villages in the new site after their old districts (omediyas). Now it was obvious they no longer wished to remain detached from the national scene, but considered themselves a vital part of it. The three villages were named with this in mind. "Sadat," the first village, was named for the president. "El Abour" (The Crossing) was the name given to the second village to commemorate the 1973 crossing of the Suez Canal by the Egyptians to regain their occupied territory in Sinai, captured in the 1967 war. The third village, "El Salam," the village of peace, honors the 1977 peace initiative taken by Sadat.

Through this symbolic use of names the Nubians hope to dramatize their actions and link them to the national political scene. As a result of their life in the Kom Ombo region, the consciousness of the Nubians has evolved to the national level. The contact with government and non-Nubian groups has resulted in an expansion of their sensitivities and has influenced their decisions and plans about the future. They can never be the same, but can only continue to expand in the direction they are going.

As an example of their determination, the Nubian Women's Association approached the president's wife and presented their cause. The association also succeeded in having her visit Kom Ombo to see the worsening situation in New Nubia. This stimulated her sympathy and interest. The president shared her concern about Nubian demands to have the government facilitate their return, and on January 14, 1979, he eventually visited with the Nubians who had moved to the lake's shores. This visit reflected the state's positive support for the Nubian cause and gave impetus to reluctant government departments to ease off their reservations in facilitating the living conditions for the Nubian returnees. He even promised the Nubians that forty-two new Nubian villages would be reconstructed on the lake's shores when Egypt began to enjoy "the prosperity of a peace era."

While the Nubians were able to collect some eighty-thousand Egyptian pounds as shares in their cooperative society, the government promised matching funds. During Sadat's visit with the Nubians at the lake, he ordered the payment of one-hundred Egyptian pounds to each Nubian settler, who numbered altogether between one and two hundred according to various reports. There were a small number of women, and President Sadat attended a Nubian wedding while he was in the region.

To dramatize the effects of the president's visit and to make the most of it, the Nubians anounced the 14th of January as a Nubian holiday; this move, as a coping strategy, assures their distinct ethnic identity and, at the same time, links them to national politics, at least a government's commitment to accommodate, more or less at this stage, their demands.

Following the presidential visit, the Cairo and Alexandria Nubian clubs, as well as the numerous village-based Nubian associations in several Egyptian cities, began to show real concern for the lake settlement. They held several meetings with officials and mobilized their members to support the move and donate money to enable the "Nubian pioneers of the lake to survive and face the challenge," in Awad's words. They also organized and sponsored trips down to the lake for inspections and as a show of support to their fellow Nubians. The youth from Cairo and Alexandria were also organized into work camps in the Abu Simbel region for the purpose of constructing roads, planting trees, and developing the region in general. Men, women, the young and the old became involved, helping to bridge the passage to the lake's shores, and "the return to the beloved land" picked up a wide support in the Nubian community as well as in government circles. "It is not anymore the dream of two elderly men," in the words of a Nubian agronomist, who, at the age of twenty-five designed a multifunctional farming project for implementation in the motherland of Nubia for his village association.

NUBIANS PLAN FOR THEMSELVES

Traditionally, projects in Egypt such as the Nubian cooperative society have stemmed from the government. The Nubians' success in raising funds and organizing social-change projects from within their own community is an extremely positive indicator of the creativity inherent in their culture since these actions are relatively new in the mechanism of financing national projects. Through their assertive actions the Nubians have developed a political tactic, or strategy, raised money from within their own communities, initiated the plans for action, and then exercised pressure on the government in order to gain support for their programs.

This is best illustrated in the formation of the cooperative society in 1977 and the success of the Nubians in obtaining financial aid from the government, which has been extremely helpful in assisting the Nubians. At times when funds were not available, the government often provided equipment, supplies, and technical assistance. The government's support is an indication of its feelings regarding the Nubian's abilities to develop and utilize resources. The Nubian return to the lake's shores and input for the plans is a rather unusual case of local development in Egypt; it deserves monitoring and periodic assessment.

The concept of growth and development is important in a spatial context, not only for the Nubians in the Kom Ombo region but for the "urban group" which is mostly concentrated in cities in the northern part of the country. Kom Ombo will probably function as a connecting point between the urban dwellers in the north and settlers of the lake region in the south. The lake settlement will link the Nubians with their Sudanese fellows, giving them new outlets and options beyond the national borders. This spatial extension will enlarge their economic opportunities, thus ensuring their human dignity by allowing them expansion and freedom of movement. Their cultural migratory patterns will continue (for it is their nature to expand and evolve); however, this small group (comprising less than 1 percent of the population) can now look more securely toward the future and need no longer fear the loss of cultural heritage.

As of 1980, the Nubians' role in development has taken a new direction, and they have demonstrated an impressive innovation. Two striking examples of such innovation are those of land and fishing-industry development. In late 1979, a Nubian undertook the task of developing, as a private enterprise, a three-hundred-acre farm for cultivation, growing fodder, and animal husbandry. This entrepreneurs' venture, which includes the services of agronomists, land planners, and others, is a striking example of development from within the private sector. His "estate farm" rather than "state farm" is symbolic of development that does not require the constant supervision by the government. Moreover, recent governmental policies in 1978 and 1979 have evolved toward encouraging such innovation, especially in the area of land development and settlement.

Regarding the lake fishing industry, it is significant that Nubians, previously not interested in fishing, have became involved with it, but as an investment rather than a subsistence measure. The government has reacted favorably to Nubian input; it has also provided loans for the purchase of boats and related equipment. Consequently, in 1979, the Nubians formed a Nubian Cooperative Society for Fishing.

FUTURE PROJECTIONS

Given the attitudes toward change that exist within the framework of the Nubian culture, there are three variables from which to draw in order to project the future. First, and most importantly, are the Nubian cultural patterns and the character and attitudes of the people; and second are the factors regarding the lake's potential development in terms of possibilities and limitations. The second variable is important as the problems related to distance, rising costs, and inadequate materials will inevitably affect the Nubians' abilities to implement their plans rapidly. Any new relocation scheme will undoubtedly involve a longer period of time and will require certain coping mechanisms that are presumably different from those already experienced in Kom Ombo.

The third variable that must be accounted for is the recently broached subject of integration; it is a political issue and is therefore particularly vulnerable to the ups and downs in the relationship between Egypt and the Sudan. In this respect the course of events is unforeseen, but one could safely predict that if the concept of integration between the two countries disappears from the political scene and enthusiasm fades for the project, the Nubians will do it their own way once they succeed in establishing a presence in the lake region.

The lake ecosystem, especially with regard to other lake residents in terms of number, ethnicity, occupation, will determine the existing nature of the new Nubian community in the lake region and its future. As of 1980, there were about eight thousand fishermen in the lake area, concentrating in its northern and middle regions. The population of the fishing community is largely male, residing on boats. As previously indicated, these people left their home villages in Upper Egypt to search for work.

Another group of people, whose number is not exactly known but is estimated to be three to four thousand, are the bedouins of the Eastern or Arabian Desert. These nomadic tribes were totally overlooked in the resettlement scheme, on the basis that they constituted an extremely small portion of the inhabitants below the Aswan Dam.

For the majority of these nomads, the formation of the lake depleted their natural resources and they, consequently, reacted by retreating deep into the Eastern Desert. Some moved to Daraw, a market town located about thirty-five kilometers north of the city of Aswan. They are likely to return to the shorelines of the lake if any significant vegetation develops in the area.

Other nomadic groups, a minority however, benefited from the lake, which has expanded their resources and encouraged sedentariness, as particularly observed in Khor Allaqi. (*Khor* is a local term for the lake's side extensions, comparable to an inlet.) The rise and fall of the water level has affected the ecology in the area, bringing about changes in certain aspects of their nomadic life. Pastureland had developed in the plains, and the nomads, previously isolated from the River Nile, moved toward these new grasslands provided by the fluctuating levels of the lake (Fahim 1981).

In addition to all these intervening and interrelated determinants of the future, unforeseen phenomena must also be considered, especially as they are related to the course of events at the domestic level of politics. For example, a change in government personnel will frequently affect the course of the implementation of a project, either accelerating or impeding the process. Governmental interest in Nubian goals will be needed to produce success in specific situations.

There will be, of course, other factors or new developments that will definitely determine the attitudes and behavior of the Nubians toward their future. Some of these aspects include their long and extensive cultural heritage, the independence they have exhibited regarding economic and political development, and the growing solidarity that has developed among them. Additionally, in searching for patterns to predict the future we should not overlook the Kom Ombo experience, which has presumably changed cultural values and thus affected the Nubians' aspirations for the future. The changes in cultural values need thorough investigation, for new interaction patterns have evolved and expanded relationships, not only with the government, but also in the context of expanding enterprises which Nubians continue to develop in the cities and abroad. Their continuing relationship with the Upper Egyptians for purposes of agricultural labor will be a continuing factor in their future.

Although an assessment of the human elements of attitude and behavior is essential in an attempt to foresee the future, several other indicators must also be observed. Population dynamics is one such important element, and it is unfortunate that no reliable demographic information is available on the Nubian returnees up to this point in time. Population growth and the age and sex composition must all be viewed as relevant, for if the elderly are eventually to be the only group returning to the lake, the new villages will soon become a refuge rather than a viable economic settlement. The question of sex composition and male absenteeism will be another indicator of stabilization within the new community. For instance, will the Nubians have primarily a male population in their new villages on the lake shores, as the fishermen do, or will the women be involved in the growth of the region as they were in Old Nubia and in the relocation process in Kom Ombo?

On the basis of this information one may assume that the Nubians will continue toward a realization of their cultural and economic motivations and goals with the maintenance of their values. These values will most assuredly change, because change is significant, providing constant growth and evolution; and what is applicable today may no longer be valid in the future, and even while clinging to old patterns and traditions people must adapt to the new realities.

Chapter Nine
Nubians Abroad and the London Case

by Katherine Helmer

To be rooted is perhaps the most important and least recognized need of the human soul. It is one of the hardest to define.

Simone Weil (1952:43)

BACKGROUND

Historically, Nubians have manifested considerable organizational capacities and political acumen in the formation of urban associations whose twofold purpose was to help migrants adapt economically and socially to the urban environment and to combine efforts to look after the needs of those left behind in Old Nubia (Fernea and Gerster 1973:39–42). Studies have demonstrated increasing cultural assimilation and social mobility among Nubians living in Egypt's urban centers (Geiser 1966), suggesting a decreasing need for the services originally provided. Associations visited in 1978 in Egypt were most active with respect to negotiations with the Egyptian government on compensation for Nubian homes and lands, and support for those wishing to return to the shores of the lake.

International migration, however, has revived the historical purposes of Nubian associations. Nubians are traveling to altogether foreign and pluralistic societies. Perhaps, as one Nubian remarked, "there is more need than ever before for an association. We are surrounded by many strange cultures and people that we cannot hope to understand."

THE EGYPTIAN NUBIAN BENEVOLENT SOCIETY OF LONDON

In 1973, eleven Nubians began the Egyptian Nubian Benevolent Society of London. By 1978, their society boasted fifty-seven members. They engaged the services of a British attorney to counsel them on legal procedures involved in the formal recognition of their society. Without formalization, they could not legally start a joint bank account, rent a house for a meeting place, or request financial backing from national and international agencies. Official recognition would open the door to these and other new activities.

The society's members are all Nubians of Egyptian nationality. They had first considered including the many Sudanese Nubians living in London, but this idea was rejected. There being many more Sudanese Nubians than Egyptian Nubians in London, the desired fifty-fifty representation of the two groups on the executive council would have been unfair to the Sudanese. The Egyptian Nubians also anticipated that differing interests, especially with regard to promoting development on their respective relocation sites might present problems. Thus, the Egyptian Nubians' concern for establishing a cohesive organization with a focused purpose led them to form an exclusively Egyptian Nubian association. All Egyptian Nubians are automatically accepted as members. By retaining the qualifier "Egyptian" in their association's title, the Nubians acknowledge their dual identity as Nubians and Egyptian citizens. The society welcomes non-Nubians from Egypt into its membership on the condition that four of the seven executive council members approve.

The association in London also bestows honorary memberships on noteworthy visitors from Egypt. In the past, businessmen in the import-export trade, radio broadcasters, and other such personalities have been guests of honor at receptions or invited on group excursions to the sea. These honorary members often contribute financial assistance to the association. Receptions are also held to honor those who have shown concern for Nubian culture through research or publications. On one occasion, Fahim and I attended a reception in honor of Elizabeth Warnock Fernea, an ethnographer and author, whose husband, Robert Fernea, conducted crucial anthropological research among the Nubians prior to their relocation. At this reception, Fahim presented a copy of Robert Fernea's book, *Nubians in Egypt* (1973), to the members. They were delighted to recognize friends and places in the beautifully illustrated book, and expressed their hopes to see more such results from research on their people.

PURPOSE OF THE ASSOCIATION

Two main goals are outlined in the society's bylaws: (1) to provide for the welfare of Nubians living in London, and (2) to form an international center for Nubians abroad who share a concern for New Nubia.

With respect to the first goal, they wish to establish a "venue" for the society. This would be a meeting place for association members and their families during social events, such as marriage and bereavement, when Nubians share moments of joy and sadness with their relatives and friends. As most of the Nubians live in bedsitters or their place of work, they need a commodious setting to receive congratulations or consolations from their fellows.

The society's quarters would also provide inexpensive rooms for Nubian countrymen. Nubians between jobs or newly arrived in London could find immediate accommodations at low cost, to be paid when the individual has a steady income.

Apart from supplying decent accommodations, the society wishes to provide for the financial security of its members. It hopes to offer repayable loans to those in need, to give financial assistance to families in case of death, and to avoid financial catastrophes by organizing insurance policies through an accredited insurance company.

The intentions of the society, as expressed in its statutes, reveal the solidarity that traditionally characterizes Nubian communities. The Egyptian Nubian Benevolent Society continues a historic pattern of community-oriented self-help.

The ideology of the association's members, however, reflects their sensitivity to the sociopolitical climate of London. As one Nubian put it, "We want to be a model immigrant group in London. We want to show the English government that we look after our own people. We will not be a burden on the government." Nubians perceive themselves as unique in terms of their concern for the welfare of kin and nonkin alike and their desire to actively ensure the well-being of all Nubians and Egyptians in London.

Nubians believe that Pakistanis and Indians in London do not care for anyone besides their own small families and that they limit interfamilial efforts to the realm of business enterprises, such as grocery stores and real estate.

On several occasions, Nubians remarked that other immigrant groups conducted themselves poorly in London. They perceive Jamaicans and West Indians as "aggressive" people who "do not know how to behave." "They would rape women. We would never do such a thing," one man remarked. Nubians see themselves in a hostile environment: Many places are unsafe for a woman; certain sections of the town are dangerous even for a man.

The second purpose of the association, as outlined in the bylaws, is to build a relationship between the London group, those associations already long-established in Egypt, and associations to be established in Western Europe. Nubians in London envision their association as a center of communication and cooperation for all Nubians working in Europe and the United States. They see their association as setting a precedent for the formation of similar societies in other countries.

One of the specific purposes of such cooperation is to assist Nubians residing in the "motherland" of New Nubia. The problems that persist on the resettlement scheme in Egypt are of special interest to older members who spent childhood days in Old Nubia and experienced the trauma of resettlement. In 1977, they hosted the then governor of Aswan during his visit to London. Holding a reception at the Savoy Court Hotel, they discussed problems remaining to be solved on the Kom Ombo site. These issues included an adequate supply of drinking water during dry periods, an adequate transportation system of the resettlement area, and hopes for seeing an expanded university program in Aswan. They also broached the topic of the present movement by Nubians to resettle along the lake's shore. The society has discussed the possibility of sending a tractor to aid pioneers returning to farm the inhospitable shores of the lake.

Nubian Employment

While many Nubians resent popular Arab stereotypes about faithful Nubian servants, in London they profit from the practical consequences of that reputation. Of the fifty-seven men employed, nearly 72 percent work for Arab government institutions, including embassies, consulates, and the offices of joint British–Arab undertakings. They serve in a variety of capacities in these institutions as housekeepers, cooks, drivers, messengers, interpreters, and clerks.

Another type of employment, involving eight men, is personal services to Arab royalty and businessmen. This work includes a variety of services as body guard, driver, messenger, etc. One Nubian described himself as a free-lancer who shows Arab dignitaries and businessmen around London in the car he has bought for these purposes.

Three Nubians work in the hotel industry, one serving as an assistant manager and two as regular employees. Another Nubian works as an agronomist.

In general, Nubians in London are filling an employment niche not easily filled by Englishmen. Their facility in Arabic, ability to establish suitable rapport with Arabs of lofty social status, and cultural affinity as fellow Muslims have secured that niche, as well as their people's historic role as cultural intermediaries in the services.

The employment niche may have affected the age structure of the group. The Nubian men range in age from twenty-three to sixty-three years. Only 66 percent are twenty-three or thirty-eight, an age group most often associated with labor migration. Perhaps the substantial representation of men over thirty-eight is due to the fact that their work is not physically taxing, and consequently, older men are equally suited to the tasks.

The availability of relatively well-paid employment in London is an advantage to the Nubians, whose home nation is unable to provide employment at comparable wages. Compared to other immigrants arriving without specialized skills, the Nubians' net incomes are appreciably higher. Residing at their place of employment, they avoid living expenses that typically diminish a migrant's earnings. Their jobs are more secure from the conservative push to tighten immigration laws in the United Kingdom because their immigration is handled through the Foreign Office in collaboration with the embassies and consulates demanding their services.

NEW TRENDS IN THE MIGRATORY PATTERN

A close relationship between the attainment of manhood and migration has long been part of Nubian culture. By the eighteenth century, Nubian men were leaving their homes in Old Nubia and migrating to the northern cities of Egypt in search of work. There are, however, significant differences in the form that Nubian migration has taken over the years, especially in view of twentieth-century migration patterns. Early patterns were presumably those of seasonal or annual circular movement to Alexandria or Cairo. Men migrated alone, leaving their wives and children with the elderly in the secluded hamlets on the Nile in Old Nubia. Date trees, small animals, and available land were tended by spouses and relatives remaining behind. Scudder (1966) has demonstrated that labor-migration rates increased as per-capita land resources decreased. Via packboats on the Nile, migrants sent mail, commodities that were not produced in Old Nubia, and small sums of money to help maintain their relatives. According to popular Nubian belief, men would work in Cairo or Alexandria for varying lengths of time and then return with their savings to Old Nubia, where they remained until their savings were spent.

Geiser (1967) suggests that this pattern changed prior to World War II, when Nubians began to make permanent homes in urban centers and brought their wives and children to live with them, returning to Old Nubia perhaps only once every ten years to see relatives left behind.

From the London data, it appears that international migration has reinstated the historic pattern of leaving one's spouse and children in the care of parents. Of the fifty-seven Nubian men, thirty-five are married, twenty-seven to Nubian women. Of those twenty-seven Nubian wives, sixteen reside in New Nubia, seven live elsewhere in Egypt, and only four live with their husbands in London. (Three Egyptian women and four women of various nationalities account for the other wives resident in London.) Two men, both in their fifties, who have been in London for over a decade, have polygamous marriages. Each man has a Nubian and a foreign wife, the former residing in New Nubia and the latter in London.

As for those not presently married, nineteen are aged twenty-three to thirty-six and three are aged forty-five to fifty-one (information on divorced or deceased spouses is lacking.) Many of the young men have received messages from home regarding marriage plans. The mother prepares a list of suitable marriage partners selected from her family or village. On his return, the young man chooses a wife from among those on the list. During one fieldwork period of twelve days, a young man left to be married in New Nubia. He did not plan to bring his bride back to London with him.

Because the Egyptian census does not differentiate between Nubians and other Egyptians living abroad or within national boundaries, it is not feasible to know exactly how many Nubians are in diaspora. According to a young Nubian visiting London from Kuwait, there is an association in Kuwait for each and every New Nubian village. For his own association in Kuwait, he estimated the membership at one thousand. Gourta, a Kenuz village divided into three residential sections in New Nubia, has five meeting places in Kuwait. This helps to explain Nubians' affectionate nickname for Kuwait: Gourta People.

The village of Gourta also figures significantly as a place of birth for the Nubians in the London association. Twenty-five members were born in Gourta, Old Nubia. An additional fourteen members were born in five other Kenuz villages of Old Nubia. Six members were born in Mahas-speaking villages of Old Nubia. Of the twelve members not born in Old Nubia, seven were born in Aswan and are Kenuz in origin. The remaining five were born in Cairo, Alexandria, and Suez.

The preponderance of men originally from Gourta or at least from the Kenuz group is not unexpected. The district of Gourta in Old Nubia displayed one of the lowest sex ratios of men to women in 1960, and its men showed a tendency to migrate greater distances in search of work. In Geiser's study (1967), there is evidence that even before relocation Gourta males had a greater propensity for international migration to places other than the Sudan. This contrasts with the tendency for the Fedija (the Mahas-speaking Nubians) to migrate to the Sudan.

The Nubians in London, as a rule, have not come directly from Egypt to London. Only eighteen Nubians had never worked abroad before coming to London. The Nubians in London represented work experiences in thirteen countries apart from England and Egypt. Three individuals have worked in as many as five foreign countries, but the average is between two and three, including Greece, France, Italy, and the United States. There is an obvious bias for work in Arab countries, e.g., Lebanon, Kuwait, Saudi Arabia. Further investigation is needed to explain the movements of individual Nubians through time or geographical areas.

Most of the men explained their departure from Egypt in terms of wage differentials between Egypt and the surrounding Arab and Mediterranean countries. Economic conditions in Egypt have worsened in the past decade bringing serious inflation in the cost of living and no corresponding rise in workers' salaries. Population growth and urbanization have outstripped the government's ability to create employment opportunities; and the service and informal sectors, long a catchall for urban immigrants, are incapable of absorbing more workers.

TIES WITH NEW NUBIA

How often do emigrants return to New Nubia? The London Nubians may not be representative of others, but the data indicate a continuing interest in their homeland. Twenty-nine of the fifty-seven men have visited New Nubia since emigrating to London. The average number of return visits per Nubian man is 1.9, and the range is from one to five trips. Those men who have made at least one trip to New Nubia have done so on an average of once every four or five years.

An average of one visit every four years is remarkable given travel costs and the number of gifts that a migrant brings home for relatives and friends. Such an average suggests a strong commitment to those left behind and substantial interest in maintaining close contact with the home community. It is also likely that many of the migrants have interests in ongoing farming operations in New Nubia.

Those who have not returned to New Nubia since their arrival in England are most often unmarried men who arrived in London after 1974. Those married men who have *not* returned are either married to non-Nubians or married to Nubian women not residing in New Nubia.

The number of visits made to New Nubia may be a deceptive index of the number of times migrants have been reunited with their families. Some Nubians and their brothers working abroad would arrange to return to Egypt at the same time; and by sending money to their parents or family for the tickets, the entire family would meet in Cairo.

Given the number of visits between London and New Nubia and among Nubians abroad, communications could be maintained without standard mail services or telephones; friends and relatives allow word-of-mouth or hand-carried messages to travel steadily and relatively quickly. However, mail services and telephones are used extensively during festive periods and at times of crisis. The following experience of one London Nubian called Mohamed, illustrates the continuing concern and communication between Nubians in Egypt and abroad:

In 1977, Mohamed's father wrote saying that he was ill and had to travel to Cairo for treatment. Mohamed's uncle in Cairo soon sent a letter to a second uncle in Bonn, Germany. This uncle in Germany telephoned Mohamed to let him know that his father was very seriously ill. Mohamed flew to Cairo and accompanied his father back to New Nubia where he soon passed away. Mohamed received 22 telegrams and 122 condolence cards and messages in London and Egypt concerning his bereavement. Many cards arrived from Saudi Arabia and Kuwait. Mohamed said that the means of communication varied with the closeness of his relationship with the others: close kin visited in person if possible, if not, they telephoned or sent telegrams; more distant relatives and friends living abroad sent messages and letters. Mohamed made a list of all those who had sent messages and answered every one. He feels obliged to get in touch with these people if something happens in their family and to send greetings on holidays.

In this section we have sketched the kind and frequency of interaction between Nubian emigrants and those Nubians remaining in New Nubia by focusing on the actions of individuals and their families. To form a more complete picture, we need to consider Nubians as members of the Egyptian Nubian Benevolent Society—and how they have pursued activities relating to New Nubia and the recent popular movement to resettle on the shores of the new lake.

As mentioned in Chapter Eight, the Nubians in 1977 formed an agricultural cooperative society for the purpose of land reclamation, cultivation, and settlement along the lake's shores. Consequently, in March 1978, an older member of the London association presented a proposal concerning the possibility of claiming land on the shores of the lake in the name of the association. He suggested that a list be made of those members buying shares at the price of 50 *irsh* per share (in 1978 an *irsh* was $.75 U.S.) and that the money be sent through a bank to Cairo, where a Nubian association would arrange for land to be bought in the name of the London association. The proposal received only partial support. Older members were more favorably disposed toward the proposition. They viewed it as a form of future security, according to one promoter. The younger members, on the other hand, were less in favor of the plan. They wanted to build upon their lives in London, instead of looking back to Egypt for investments and future plans. If investments were made on the lake, they preferred investing in the Abu Simbel tourist industry to buying land or sending back agricultural equipment, such as tractors. Due to the split in the membership, the association did not go ahead with the proposition. Nonetheless, approximately half of the membership sent money to their families in Egypt to buy shares on a family basis.

The fate of this proposition is indicative of the differences in perspective between older and younger members. Farming appears to signify the past for the young; leaving the land is a sign of progress and modernization. According to one member, these differences are not simply a matter of age. They pertain, rather, to the fact that those who were not raised in Old Nubia "are not Nubian in outlook or mentality. They are not communal in spirit, and tend to forget their responsibility to look after the people back home."

A NUBIAN FAMILY IN LONDON

This section is a complement to preceding ones, which have given a preliminary description of members of the Nubian society. By conveying neighborhood scenes, homelife, and the personal experiences of one Nubian family in London, the data take on a human dimension . . . and the story is told.

We conducted much of our research in the area of Earl's Court (Southwest London), which some Londoners have nicknamed "Mecca." To a visitor strolling on Earl's Court, the sobriquet seems well-earned. Arab dialects are overheard in passing; sidewalks are crowded with tourists and immigrants from the East; women from the Gulf regions and Saudi Arabia wearing their distinctive veils enter grocery stores with their families.

Earl's Court caters to tourists. Three banks are available for money changing at odd hours of the day and night. The hungry flock to a number of ethnic restaurants, including three kebab shops, an expensive Turkish restaurant, and others offering Chinese, Italian, and Spanish cuisine. Several stores specialize in merchandise appealing to travelers, such as camera equipment, luggage, fine shoes and clothes.

At night, Earl's Court comes alive with the clientele of its many pubs, taverns, and nightclubs, which display pictures of Middle Eastern dancers and orchestras. Youths emerge from the underground station to find nearby student hostels.

Although tourists pump life into Earl's Court, there are also small businesses to serve neighborhood residents. Butcher shops advertise (in Arabic) that their meat is slaughtered according to Islamic law.

It is in this area that the Nubians we met had first rented a meeting place; they were soon asked to leave because the old building that housed the apartment was to be torn down. Several Nubians have lived and still live in the area, although many reside at their place of employment. It is also in this area where, during two visits to London, I spent much time in the company of one particular family whose generous hospitality, friendship, and strength were admirable. What follows is a description of this family and their life in London. (Their names have been changed.)

Ali, his wife Laila and their daughter Malika are struggling to cope with life in a foreign country. Ali, an officer of the Nubian association, is highly sensitive to the changes in the Nubian people's social conditions and culture. He has experienced childhood in Old Nubia; resettlement in 1963; and life in Aswan, Cairo, West Germany, and London. Laila is one of only four Nubian women who have migrated to live with their husbands. Although Laila does not complain, our conversations together helped me understand the difficulties and loneliness that migration can bring to women. Their seven-year-old daughter Malika is just beginning school, the first step in her adjustment to city life and a foreign culture that she eagerly emulates.

Ali and his family live in a bedsitter in a three-story apartment building on a busy highway perpendicular to Earl's Court. The landlord is slowly making improvements in the building, adding another common bathroom to service the four bedsitters on the top two floors. Ali and Laila are embarrassed by the state of the building and hope to find an apartment in the near future that will afford them more space and privacy. Their home in New Nubia was spacious and warmed by the sun. Indeed, foreigners curious about Nubian culture were sometimes brought to their home to view its fine example. Their bedsitter, nevertheless, is neat and tidy, albeit somewhat crowded when evening visitors converge all at once. Their friends can always find a place on the small couch, large bed, or small chairs that line the walls and take up most of the floor space in their one room. A large color television with remote control and a combination radio–cassette-recorder provide entertainment for guests if the conversation lulls.

A sign of the change in their lives: On the walls are counterposed a postcard of a fair-headed English family relaxing in their luxurious living-room and a pair of pictures, one of a young Arab in a fez smoking a water pipe and another of a charming Arab beauty adorned with gold. Laila shows pictures taken in New Nubia of herself and Ali, and tells me the proper names for earrings, necklaces, and head pieces. She had to leave them all behind. If not for their characteristic smiles and poise, it would be difficult to recognize them in London as Nubians. Ali long ago abandoned his galabia and turban; he wears a three-piece suit, while Laila dons British housedresses and sometimes a wig.

When Ali and Laila were married in 1970, they never imagined they would find themselves in London. Laila had been raised in Cairo. At sixteen she left for New Nubia, and at nineteen she became officially engaged to Ali. (Laila, Ali's paternal cousin, said she knew whom she would marry by the time she was ten years old.) Living with his parents in New Nubia, Ali and Laila enjoyed one year together after their marriage. During this time Malika was born.

Although Ali had completed training as a lathe specialist in an Aswan trade school, no jobs were available, and he was put on a long waiting list. Meanwhile, he learned welding at a youth center in Aswan. In 1971, he left for West Germany to work in a factory that could use his skills. A year later he was asked to leave; the tragic 1972 Olympics had made the German government wary of Arab guest workers, and there was pressure to hire nationals. After returning to New Nubia for a short visit with his wife and family, Ali left for England. Laila cried constantly about his absence. His visits and weekly letters were a comfort, but as Ali remarked, "We wanted to live our young lives together." So, in 1977, four years after his arrival in London, he managed to bring his wife and child to London.

Ali and Laila were not without family in this new city. Their most frequent visitors were Ali's brother Mohamed, sometimes accompanied by his Scottish bride Laura, and their cousins Hussein and Fatima.

The latter, another pair of married cousins, had brought a small child with them and had left the older one with grandparents in New Nubia.

Newly arrived in London, the two couples went dancing and sightseeing on weekends. Within a few months, the outings came to an end; Laila and Fatima found that they were both pregnant and, in their discomfort, they no longer wanted to venture out so often. They stopped attending government English courses for foreigners, and their husbands tried to teach them the rudiments at home after a tiring day at work.

Although Ali and Laila are glad to be together again, the move to London has entailed many sacrifices on both their parts. Laila spends many days home alone while Malika is at school. Unable to speak English, she feels vulnerable outside her home. She remembers the day she fainted on the street while bringing Malika home from school and their inability to make themselves understood to solicitous bystanders. She does not phone her friends because they share telephones with tenants who cannot understand her. In New Nubia, Laila never lacked for good company: Friends were always arriving for tea or to help with the household chores. Child care was shared with female relatives and neighbors. Laila had a sewing machine to make dresses for family use or for sale. Now she suffers from the monotony of living in a small apartment with little to do and no one to do it with.

Ali has taken charge of many duties that would normally fall on Laila's shoulders. He does the grocery shopping and accompanies Malika to school. These tasks require some fluency in English and familiarity with the city. During my first visit, Laila was ill, and Ali often helped prepare food and tea for guests. Accustomed to going out at night, Ali now seldom leaves after supper unless Laila has company. She feels insecure living in a building with so many foreigners.

Little Malika grows restless in their apartment. Raised in New Nubia among Kanzi speakers, she never learned Egyptian Arabic. Her parents try to speak it at home so she will be fluent when they return to Egypt. Her classmates in school are both immigrant and English children, and she is quickly learning English. Malika is applying herself to the language with the enthusiasm of a young child playing a new game. She practices the English alphabet at home on a magnetic board her father bought. Even on a walk to the park, she brings her school books and says vocabulary words to herself while pointing to pictures. Malika has not forgotten her former home; her little drawings portray life back in Nubia—a home, palm trees, and a sun above. Enveloped in the British school world, she will probably adapt quickly to the culture that surrounds her family. Laila says that when the time comes Malika may marry anyone she pleases, be he Nubian or British.

When Laila and Malika receive company their eyes brighten, and they busy themselves with the preparation of tea. After it is served, conversations often turn to the health of their children. During the winter months, Nubian mothers prefer to stay inside rather than risk the cold journey to a friend's home. They fear that the harsh winter winds and snows are harmful to their children's health. Experiences with British health-care facilities are a favorite topic of conversation. In New Nubia, they had been reluctant to enter an Egyptian clinic; their children were delivered at home with a doctor or midwife in attendance. In London, they plan to give birth in a hospital because they have more confidence in British doctors and medical services. Nonetheless, they miss their mothers who offered advice and comfort during their confinement. While they are apprehensive about the experience, the arrival of a newborn will qualify their family for special government housing. Even the birth of a child has taken on a new meaning.

If other Nubian women join their husbands in London, they will face many of the same difficulties as Laila has. These are not settling-in problems that will disappear with time. Major obstacles are in the path of her personal and social adjustment to life in London; the most important single barrier is the language. If Laila could consistently attend government language courses, she might in time overcome this problem. It is likely, however, that the arrival of their new child, and others in the future, will keep her from attending such classes. Consequently, she will continue to be intimidated by the city, and Ali will remain responsible for all activities outside the home. Remaining home, in itself, is not an unhappy prospect in Laila's eyes, but passing days at home without the pleasant company of friends and relatives may be much more difficult for her to contend with.

Young Nubian bachelors are aware of the hardships of family life as represented by this couple. During the evening visit of some young friends to Ali's home, one young man half-jokingly remarked that having seen the time Ali devotes to taking care of his family, he would never bring his own to London and give up what little freedom he has.

Ali and Laila, on the other hand, consider their situation as temporary and have plans to return to Egypt. Like Laila, Ali is saddened by the distance between himself and his family. His two brothers work in Saudi Arabia; his widowed mother, two married sisters, and youngest brother live in New Nubia. Family relationships are limited to letters and remittances. "It helps them to forgive our absence," Ali said, "if we send presents of money. This is our way of sharing, but sharing means other things besides money—helping at weddings, mourning together, meeting each other at the guest house— things we cannot share when we are away."

Ali and Laila's plans to return to Egypt remain indefinite, hinged on their ability to save enough money to assure a good life in their native home. "We must remain abroad," Ali said, "in order to build a permanent life in Egypt. Life is moving, but not for all our lives will we be immigrants. You can live in Germany or England for years, but you cannot forget your home. As long as we live here we must go back to New Nubia. Throughout time, generations have returned."

We hope that Ali and Laila succeed. In certain ways they exemplify the situation of many Nubian families who left their homelands and families in search of a better future. As part of a community that over the centuries has developed effective ways of dealing with migration, they may have a much better chance of reaching their goal.

COMMENTARY (by H. M. Fahim)

Although my London visits with the Nubians were peripheral in nature and did not constitute part of my ongoing research on the dynamics of the Nubian resettlement, I have come to consider international migration among the Nubians as a significant research dimension in the overall resettlement process and its effects on the traditional culture of the relocatees.

In terms of the methodology and objectives of doing research among Nubian migrants in Europe, I have found the work done by James Watson (1974, 1975) interesting and relevant. In 1971, he studied Chinese restaurant workers in London, who emigrated from the village of San Tin where he had been involved previously in fieldwork. Like Watson, we had no one research site in London; we met with the Nubians wherever we had access to them. Unlike the San Tin people, who had not formed a village association or held periodic gatherings, the Nubians were a formally organized group. Helmer and I were fortunate enough to meet with most of the Nubians in just a few days after initial contact with one person, a cook at the Egyptian Embassy.

Examining the case of Nubians in London in the context of Watson's studies, several interesting comparative and theoretical issues have emerged. For instance, Helmer and I found that the Nubians in London, like the Mans from San Tin, send remittances to their families back home. Some Nubians stated that they sometimes send up to one-fourth of their income, especially on festive and social occasions. These remittances that flow to New Nubia from abroad constitute an important income source for Nubian families. Because of the high rate for hard-currency exchange in Egypt, they have improved Nubian living standards, as evidenced by their use to acquire modern furniture and electrical appliances.

Some Nubians felt that the apparent financial benefits of working abroad might result in a significant change in the age at which youngsters begin thinking about leaving for work outside Nubia. They fear that the glamour of travelling abroad and the lure of large earnings in hard currency will weaken the perceived value of an education. Nubians have promoted and encouraged their children's education since resettlement as a strategy to meet competition in their new environment.

Their concerns may be well-founded. With reference to the Mans of San Tin who had emigrated from Hong Kong, Watson wrote of an "educational crisis." He observed that "in striking contrast to other parts of Hong Kong, academic motivation is low in San Tin. The children are not convinced that education is a necessity because they see semiliterate returnees building sterling houses and driving automobiles. They also realize that the only qualification needed for employment in the high-paying restaurants abroad is membership in the Man Lineage. Many of the adolescents drop out before they finish the six forms (grades) of primary school and wait idly, sometimes for years, until they are old enough to obtain vouchers or work permits" (1975:192–93).

In terms of the effects of international migration on the traditional culture and its presumed role in bringing about radical change in the original homeland of the migrants, Watson found that "emigration was not a force for modernizing San Tin, but a means for reasserting many traditional values." He observed in the village that "the returned emigrants themselves generally do not act as change agents, and after their retirement they often become the most enthusiastic proponents of traditional values" (1974:221).

Whether this applies to the Nubian case is a researchable question. It is interesting to note that some Nubians abroad, two of whom are now working in the United States, are enthusiastic advocates and supporters of the Society for Revival of Nubian Heritage, established in Cairo in 1980. Does this mean that outside sources of money and steady remitttance incomes have allowed Nubians to emulate some of the highest ideals of their cultural heritage as has been the case for the Mans of San Tin (Watson 1975:216)? Does this also suggest the development of a dual attitude among all emigrants, that is, to be relatively liberal and susceptible to change in diaspora while retaining conservatism and traditionalism back home? Does the fact that the emigrants know of their eventual return to their homeland make them develop such a dual strategy to cope with the requirements of both old and new ways of life? Watson concluded that "the goal of most San Tin emigrants is not urban assimilation but a triumphant return to their home village where they hope to retire in comfort with their savings" (1974:201). We found a similar attitude among the Nubians in London.

In a recent volume edited by Coelho and Ahmed, issues of migration, adjustment, and change have been thoroughly explored in a psychological/sociological context. They viewed migration, in all its types, as a state of uprooting, which they labelled as "the crucial metaphor" of modernization and assumed that it would be the dominant trend underlying much social change (1980:xiii). This might be true, but another question emerges. Does change in the emigrants' world view, character, and life-style bring about a corresponding change in the home community at large?

PART IV
RESEARCH, THEORY, AND POLICY

United Nations sociologist Raymond Apthorp describes planned settlements as "experiments in nation-building in miniature" (Tadros 1980:1); and it is difficult enough to analyze, plan, implement, and manage the technical aspects of land reclamation and settlement. As Waterbury concludes from a 1971 workshop on "Human Settlements on New Lands" (see El Hamamsy and Garrison 1979), "the dangers are myriad: Projects can be engulfed by sand, rendered useless because of inadequate drainage and soil salinity, unsuited for the kinds of crops planned for them because of faulty soil research, or atrophied because related aspects of physical planning, such as the building of access roads and procedures for marketing produce, were not integrated into the original plan" (Waterbury 1972:3). But physical planning and costing may be a relatively simple matter compared to the social planning upon which the project's viability will ultimately depend. The nexus of social challenges encompasses a gamut of little-understood problems of ordinary motivation, commitment, and capacity to learn.

Because of this complexity, it is not surprising that research in Egypt or elsewhere continues to document more disappointments than successes with planned settlements. Indeed, the failure rate for all types of government-sponsored land-settlement projects in new lands has been discouragingly high throughout the world. Planners must seriously consider the implications of this record. Because settlement programs possess a utopian appeal, reflect certain social goals at the national level, and present a tempting opportunity to design something from scratch, planners continue to advocate ambitious new settlement

153

programs without sufficiently considering a variety of other less spectacular but perhaps more realistic alternatives.

According to Scudder (1980), recent studies indicate that the peasant is more innovative than his image may suggest, and his ancient ways contain a great deal of folk wisdom that governments and international planners must stop scorning and start adapting. While it is still fashionable for planners and administrators to lambaste the peasant, the social scientist has switched his attention to the settlement planner and administrator. Because new land settlements are planned from above, one must, in Palmer's words, "lay the blame for the preponderance of failures to the scheme planners" (1974:268). Although social researchers are not interested in placing blame in one place or another, they should, nonetheless, study settlement projects as complex systems that include not just the settler and his surroundings but also the settlement organization.

Much attention has been directed toward resettlement research and theorization. Scudder (1973) in particular has outlined a predictive model on how people respond to compulsory relocation. In several other papers, Scudder addressed himself to the policy implications of resettlement-theorization (e.g., 1976, 1980); and he has since published a developmental framework for land settlement schemes, whether compulsory or voluntary, in which he concluded that these schemes throughout the world constitute a distinctive type of subsystem which must pass through a series of developmental stages before they can be considered economically and socially viable. These stages are: (1) planning, infrastructural development, and settler recruitment; (2) transition; (3) economic and social development; and (4) handing over and incorporation (1981:9–15). Most recently, Scudder and Colson have summarized current knowledge relating to compulsory relocation (1982).

Other researchers have also been involved in resettlement studies. Though not a long-term study, Butcher's work at Volta (Ghana) and his experience with Kossou (Ivory Coast) are directly reflected in his resettlement manual (1971). An anthropology of resettlement developed, and a significant number of cases have been described (e.g., Smock 1967; Chambers 1969; Palmer 1974; Hansen and Oliver-Smith 1982), government policies evaluated, and hypotheses on how people respond to forced relocation formulated and tested. Both the World

Bank 1978 Issue Paper on "Agricultural land settlement" and the 1979 Memorandum on "Social issues associated with involuntary resettlement in bank financial projects" draw heavily on anthropological studies and their conclusions.

The Bank addressed basic issues related specifically to land resettlement schemes and made it explicit that "when development projects cause people to be compulsorily displaced, the Bank's general policy is to help the borrower to ensure, to the extent possible, that after a reasonable transition period, the displaced people regain at least their previous standards of living, and that they be economically and socially integrated into the host communities. Planning and financing the resettlement should be an integral part of the project, and the measures to be taken in this regard should be clarified before, and agreed upon during loan negotiations."

In addition to these individual efforts in the area of resettlement research, I should indicate that in several recent international conferences on water resource and land development, the resettlement component received considerable attention. Resettlement aspects, problems, and development potential have been studied by specialists in the fields of sociology, anthropology, public health, and agricultural economics. In the past decade, for instance, I have become acquainted with and participated in several international conferences which dealt with resettlement issues (e.g., Ackermann, White, and Worthington 1973; Stanley and Alpers 1975; United Nations 1976; Driver and Wunderlich 1979; El Hamamsy and Garrison 1979).

Throughout the book, several points of theoretical interest as well as potential policy issues have been directly or implicitly discussed, making the study of Nubian resettlement significantly important to present and future relocation schemes whether in Egypt or elsewhere. Nonetheless, I draw, in Chapter Ten, upon my research among the Nubians and consultancy work for the World Bank to present selected resettlement issues and discuss their related policy implications. In Chapter Eleven I present notes and reflections on my research experience among the Nubians. The main ideas in this chapter were presented in a lecture on February 25, 1976, at the New York headquarters of the Wenner-Gren Foundation for Anthropological Research. An abbreviated version of the lecture was published in the 1977 Spring issue of Human Organization.

Despite the strong criticism in anthropological literature of the "personal approach" in cultural anthropological research and the argument by some who advocate "a mixing approach" that accommodates both objective and subjective perspectives or, in other words, the standardized and humanistic methods (Honigman 1976:243), I found it difficult throughout my research work to be detached. At times my state of mind and sociopolitical views did affect my research work among the Nubians in terms of data collection and analysis.

In spite of the fact that considerable research has already been carried out in connection with human settlements on new lands in Egypt and elsewhere, comparatively little of this has been utilized by planners (Fahim and Scudder 1981). In order to examine this serious problem of inadequate utilization of research results, my experience at the Social Research Center of the American University in Cairo may provide some clues concerning social research and national development in Egypt.

The Social Research Center has been involved for several years in research on human aspects related to the establishment and management of land settlement schemes in Egypt. The Center's main objective has been the study of development issues with the dual purpose of contributing to social science knowledge and providing analyses of service to Egypt's developmental efforts. The Center is also concerned with the problems of communication between researchers and planners/ administrators. Along this line and because of the need for comparative social studies of numerous land settlement experiments in progress in Egypt and in other Middle Eastern countries, the Center organized, in September 1971, a regional workshop on the planning and development of new rural settlements (El Hamamsy and Garrison 1979).

Following the workshop and during a four-year period, the Center, in collaboration with the Egyptian Authority for the Cultivation and Development of Reclaimed Lands, undertook a study on and made an evaluation of the rehabilitation process in the newly settled communities in land reclamation areas. This study had two main objectives: The first was to provide systematic information on the design and implementation of planned rural settlements; the second was to describe and analyze the rehabilitation process and associated problems in relation to socioeconomic development. Two major areas, the northwestern section of the Nile Delta and New Nubia in the Kom Ombo region, were chosen as research sites. Reports on the two components of this study were prepared (Fahim 1971, 1972a, 1975; Tadros 1975) and submitted to the Egyptian Authority for the Cultivation and Development of Reclaimed Lands and the former U.S. Health, Education, and Welfare Department, which funded the undertaking of this research (Fahim and Scudder 1981).

Chapter Ten
Some Resettlement Issues

*The issue . . . is not whether we know enough; the real questions
are whether we have the courage to say and use what we know
and whether anyone knows more.*

Alvin Gouldner (1964:205)

BACKGROUND

The displacement of the Nubian community was conceived as a
manageable social cost compared to the benefits that the construction
of the Aswan High Dam would yield. Nonetheless, experience from
the Nubian case and other resettlement schemes in Africa has clearly
indicated a failure on the part of the planners to conceive properly the
magnitude of the resettlement operation in terms of cost, time, and
management. The complexity of resettlement projects has been repeatedly emphasized in the literature. Also, the need for a long-term
perspective on planning and monitoring proved to be essential. However, as a United Nations advisor reports, "there have been cases
where a new land settlement has been treated as a once-and-for-all
occurrence: People have been settled, nothing more; or it has been
calculated that if the settlers continue to perform certain production
tasks in certain ways, they will reach a satisfactory level of living after
some years" (Jansson 1979).

The process of resettlement schemes includes four major stages or
phases including, in sequence, the scheme's conceptualization, planning, implementation, and follow-up. With respect to the Nubian
experience these phases are interrelated, and should be conceived as

159

an integrated unit and must therefore be subject to careful planning, adequate preparation, and appropriate timing. The complexity of resettlement also lies in the many variables involved in each phase and in the time framework. In several resettlement cases, though, including the Nubian, much of the planning had been statically oriented, resulting in persistent problems in the long run, especially those related to the build-up of the resettled community and the expansion and growth of its economic resources.

Literature on resettlement has identified quite a few major issues on both theoretical and policy grounds. For instance, the 1971 international workshop on "Human Settlements on New Lands" addressed issues pertinent to land development and resettlement schemes, including planning, means of implementation, and community building problems (El Hamamsy and Garrison 1979). In her introduction to the published proceedings, El Hamamsy indicated that "experience has shown that whereas, by and large, the technical problems associated with land improvement and development pose no insurmountable difficulties, the human problems associated with the planning and evolution of new settlements continue to present a challenge. The main task still facing planners is how to design the future shape of a settlement — its physical, economic, social, political, and administrative components — in such a way as to meet the needs of its future inhabitants and at the same time achieve the goals of development. The critical issue for administrators is how to help evolve socially, economically, and politically viable communities out of previously unrelated families and groups or, as in the case of involuntary resettlements, out of people deeply traumatized by the loss of their familiar habitat" (1979:vi).

SOCIAL COST AND COMPENSATION POLICIES

Nubian relocation may be looked upon as a social cost of the Aswan High Dam, and much time and energy have been lost in the rehabilitation period that the Nubians experienced. One of the negative aspects of this period for the Egyptian Nubians was the breakdown of neighborhood, family, and kinship ties due to unsatisfactory housing arrangements made by the government. Another aspect involved social benefits to be achieved by the relocation program: that of bringing an isolated rural group into the mainstream of national life. In this regard, and in the case of the Egyptian Nubians, the move represented a step upward on cultural and political levels. It provided them with a new image and new role to play in the local affairs and politics of the region. The move also made it easier for the rural and urban groups (separated because of male labor migration) to maintain more frequent contact, thus improving family ties and increasing group solidarity. Such is not the case, for instance, with the Sudanese Nubians, who view their relocation as a setback, both socially and culturally.

The fact that resettlement usually implies a social cost to the relocatees has been well perceived by the planners, and provisions have been included for a fair compensation. Social cost in resettlement schemes is not, however, an absolute; its magnitude varies with each scheme, depending on the degree of behavior modification and adaptation required in a new environment. In these terms, the social cost among the Sudanese Nubians has been much greater than that among Egyptian Nubians. In some cases, resettlement should cause a relatively small amount of stress and, by extension, should incur less social cost than other schemes that necessitate a move to an entirely different habitat and a life under completely different social and economic conditions. Consequently, I suggest that the notion of social cost be toned down and, instead, that the resettlement administration emphasize the social benefits resettlement has brought about. Otherwise, the implementation of the resettlement plan may be hindered by further demands by the relocatees, who present their agreement to relocate as an act of sacrifice and patriotism. In the case of the Kpong Hydroelectric Project in Ghana, for instance, this attitude is expressed in the words of the paramount chief of one affected village when he writes in a letter addressed to the resettlement officer of "the patriotism which the Torgome people showed in offering their lands and trees for the national welfare" (Fahim 1979a).

I believe it is important that resettlement officials make it quite clear to the relocatees that compensation for their social cost is not an endless matter. With reference again to the Kpong case, an attitude to exploit the notion of social cost and patriotism is apparent in the most recent demand of the Torgome villagers for an extension of the food aid period from two weeks to two years. I am not here dismissing the suffering that displacement may cause, but the point is that people differ in their attitudes and responses to relocation, and there are also variations regarding the intensity and duration of stress and suffering which in any case happen. Compensation policies are relative and situational and should not be viewed as a standard measure in all cases. My recommendation, therefore, is that the resettlement administration might better stress at what stage the plan has paid its dues and try to orient the relocatees toward a more participatory role in coping with displacement and autonomously developing viable communities. One condition, though, would have to be that the resettlement plan is implemented as designed and on schedule; otherwise, the relocatees may never feel compensated and could possibly become dependent on the government.

Whatever the extent of social cost may be, it is also important, as Elizabeth Colson pointed out to me, that resettlement analysts should keep officials and those involved in planning large projects aware that they are likely to cause enormous suffering to the people who have to move. These people may gain in the long run if they survive, but it is essential, still in Colson's words, to be aware what the impact will be at different stages in the process of relocation.

Food Aid and Possible Negative Implications

In most resettlement situations, the relocatees usually need an immediate food relief which enables them to cope with the initial economic hardship resulting, as has often been the case, from the unreadiness of the relocation area to support them adequately. The relocation authority should provide such food relief from its local resources, as it did in the Kainji (Nigeria) and Kariba (Zambia and Rhodesia) projects; but in most cases aid is requested from the United Nations' World Food Program (WPF), as happened in Nubia and Ghana. The time food aid is needed should be the period between the actual evacuation and the production of the first harvests, as Butcher (1971) states in his operational manual for resettlement schemes.

In my view the problem occurs in most resettlement cases because it may take years before the first harvests become possible. While this transitional period should be as short as possible, the history of African relocation projects shows that it has lasted in some areas beyond expectations. One possible serious consequence resulting from a long transitional period is the development of a dependency syndrome among the relocatees. Should food aid be extended either as a relief measure or an incentive policy during the transitional period, it can have dysfunctional effects on development. One dysfunctional effect, I presume, is not only an increasing and intensifying dependency of the relocatees on the government for food (thus hindering or at least prolonging their adjustment process), but also the creation of a dependency of local governments on international donor organizations for food aid to alleviate potential cases of starvation. International agencies should, therefore, set certain conditions and closely monitor progress in getting new lands adequately productive during the immediate years following resettlement.

With reference to the Kpong resettlement in Ghana, which was completed in 1981, Len Allen, chief engineer at ACRES, the company in charge of both the construction of the dam and the relocation scheme, reported (personal communication, November 1981) the following: "Kpong resettlement came out alright in the end with no food aid necessary. My general impression is that the VRA [Volta River Authority] put perhaps more into it than the people themselves; that is, I would have liked to have seen more willingness of the resettlers to take advantage of the new opportunities that resettlement offered. However, VRA did their part and I am advised that slowly, the people will adjust in a positive manner in their own good time."

While it is undoubtedly good news that no food aid was necessary, it is unfortunate that people still are not assuming more involvement and participation, an important resettlement issue which will be examined in a later section of this chapter.

Coping with Resettlement and Development Policies

In their survey article on resettlement, Scudder and Colson suggested that "communities undergoing forced relocation constitute a special type of social situation" in which people first "respond as if they lived in a closed sociocultural system." Following this initial stage of transition, they begin to respond "as members of an increasingly open ended and dynamic coping system" (Scudder and Colson 1982: 267). The major policy implication of such a sequential response is that the relocatees tend to resent innovations, and it is therefore advisable to introduce major economic and social changes only after the relocatees show signs of adjustment to resettlement. In other words, as Butcher has pointed out (1971:6–7), resettlement and development should be kept apart as separate processes.

Although my observations among the Nubians agree with Scudder and Colson's conclusion that the relocatees change as much as is necessary to continue behaving in accordance with pre-relocation values and goals, I still recognize the possibility of many innovations occurring, although perhaps on a limited scale, during the transitional period when stress is paramount and the relocatees find themselves faced with complex, numerous challenges and if the transitional period continues beyond the expected limited period. It is correct to assume that relocatees often adopt an "involuted strategy," to use Scudder's phrase (1973:469), yet it is also feasible that they will bring about basic changes on certain issues even if the transitional period is still on.

As a matter of fact, I observed the Nubians in the early years following resettlement practicing what I label "a dual coping strategy." By this I mean that during the transitional period Nubians acted conservatively and at the same time were innovative enough to cope positively with the aftermath of relocation. In other words, Scudder's sequential model of a conservative stance followed by an open-ended attitude for change may overlap or coexist during the immediate years after displacement, as has been demonstrated in the Nubian experience.

While it may seem a sound policy strategy to separate resettlement and development—a suggestion that presumably would ease the stress and help relocatees stand on their feet prior to their involvement in major and complex changes—it may also be an impractical measure because development constitutes an integral component of resettlement and relates to national politics. Anyway, the problem lies, in my view, not in the timing of introducing development but rather in its efficient planning and careful implementation, especially as related to social management aspects.

Resettlement Propaganda Pitfalls

Governments may commit themselves to great promises to reward the affected people (in connection with forced relocation schemes, which people often resent) for their sacrifices in the national interest. Government promises, which often create great expectations among the relocatees, are openly expressed in public speeches by officials. They are also, implicitly or explicitly, expressed in attractive pamphlets and printed matter, with photographs, describing the prosperous life in the new resettlement areas. During the period between announcement of the relocation plans and the time when the relocatees feel settled, they often expect that the government (or the relocation authority) will take over the major responsibilities for their rehabilitation. The rehabilitation period should, in principle, be kept to the absolute minimum; otherwise, a dependency syndrome can develop.

In connection with the Nubian case, these government resettlement "propaganda pitfalls" and the delays in getting the relocation area adequately productive during the years immediately following resettlement have resulted (among other factors) in prolonging the transitional period and the development of a dependency syndrome. This dependency probably can be minimized if governments make it clear to relocatees that, for example, achieving "stability, prosperity, and a decent life" (words used by the Egyptian vice-president in a speech to Nubians in January 1960) is not the government's responsibility exclusively.

Also desirable is the implementation of orientation programs to educate relocatees about resettlement and its anticipated consequences. Such a program, to be incorporated prior to the move, would provide relocatees with insights and guidelines to achieve a smoother and more rapid adjustment than that which would come from a trial-and-error approach. This would be especially useful in the area of economics to discourage such habits as unwise spending, particularly of compensation money, which has been observed among the relocated Egyptian Nubians. Information relative to the wise investment of compensation and other monies—investments that would be recycled into the new community, for example—would be most useful.

The role of the people should also be spelled out and emphasized in order to promote a feeling of shared responsibilities and to induce local initiatives. The relocatees, of course, should be acknowledged, and some appreciation shown for their sacrifices in the national interest; but they also ought to be aware that the government is only able to help them regain a normal life. Commenting on the tremendous number of Nubian complaints, a top official once made the point that "the government is now trapped by its previous promises, which made Nubians believe that it would carry them on its shoulders rather than just helping them to stand up once again." Government promises should be reasonable enough to fulfill the expectations they arouse. This implies, of course, the necessity of meeting the relocatees' minimum expectations of having their new homeland economically and socially ready within the shortest possible time to enable them to regain both their ethnic identity and self-sufficiency.

But how many years must elapse before self-sufficiency is achieved? George Foster believes that although few resettlement schemes are sufficiently old enough to provide empirical evidence, the development of self-sufficiency usually takes a very long time. In his statement on the workshop on "Human Settlement in New Lands" held in Cairo in 1971, he points out that "the question that haunted some workshop participants is whether in fact, once a deep dependency relationship is established, as in the case of village relocations, can this relationship ever be broken?" The evidence suggests, according to Foster, "that this is not possible as once an individual becomes dependent, the odds are that he or she will be more or less continuously dependent for life" (1979:61–62). Nonetheless, to minimize the dangers of permanent dependency in resettlement the establishment of a solid economic viability of the new community is a *must*.

An early build-up of the relocatees' capacity for self-sufficiency is crucial to the development of an adaptive state of mind. This is always linked to the development of economic production systems, which ultimately will provide a state of economic self-sufficiency as well as an increase in income and a diversity of sources. It is unfortunate that, as Scudder and Colson point out, almost universally "governments fail to pay proper attention to how relocatees are going to make a living after removal, scarce funds all too often being expended on housing and social services at the expense of job training and job opportunities. This makes a mockery of stated intentions to use relocation as a development strategy" (1982:270).

Related to the economic and social viability of the settler's community is the need to consider seriously the position of women and growing children. In many cases, planners have looked at the settlers' community only in terms of male adults. They, therefore, overlooked how wives and children can share in scheme benefits. Separate economic activities for women are rarely built into projects. As a result, according to Scudder, "the status of women in a number of government-sponsored settlement schemes in different parts of the world has actually deteriorated. Partly this is because it is easier for the male head of the household, who is more apt to control family finances, to keep up kinship ties by periodically returning to the old habitat; partly it is because both national and international planners tend to view settlements not as communities or farming units but rather as composed of individual farmers. Applicable, for example, to World Bank schemes in Zambia, Nepal, and Malaysia, this attitude strongly favors the male head of household. In some schemes, the wife may be evicted when her husband dies; in most, planners pay little consideration to her other than as a source of labor. Hence few schemes are concerned with how wives and children can share in scheme benefits and few schemes plan cash generating enterprises for wives and widows" (1979:17).

The subject of the next generation is also a significant resettlement issue. Egyptian Nubians, for instance, have invested in educating their children over the past years, not to "have them till the land" (as several informants have indicated) but to seek "decent jobs" in cities and, hopefully, in other Arab countries. (When they were asked about the nature of "decent jobs," the answer unanimously emphasized "secure income.") In this regard, a significant policy issue should relate to the "handing over" stage, when the male family head, by reason of death or disability, relinquishes his land responsibilities to women and/or children. It is also apparent that land settlement planners and researchers should look at these schemes as an on-going activity and should be as concerned for the future as they are for the present (Fahim and Scudder 1981).

RESETTLEMENT MANAGEMENT

Organization. The organizational part of management is the crux of most resettlement problems. It relates to capital, investment, equipment, personnel, and an entire system of bureaucracy. Governments very often, as was the case with the Nubians, form new administrative bodies or agencies to take over the entire responsibility for planning and executing resettlement and related socioeconomic development projects. Governments usually grant such organizations independent authority and the freedom to overlook established bureaucratic procedures. In practice, however, resettlement administration cannot rid itself entirely of procedural red tape, as it eventually becomes part of the total administrative machinery of the country. The top executives are themselves government bureaucrats, in addition to the fact that the resettlement administration cannot operate without contacts and coordination with other government departments. Experience with the Nubian case has shown that resettlement management, especially in connection with agricultural development, has been extremely difficult, time consuming, and may be ultimately unrewarding. Resettlement management, in my view, requires a certain caliber of personnel who must receive, whatever their job level may be, a thorough education on resettlement problems; they should go through periodic field training as well. As in the Nubian case, much of the individual stress of the relocatees was caused by lack of understanding on the part of the resettlement planners and administrators as well as inefficient communication between the two groups.

Understanding the problems of the field resettlement administrators is also essential. Although the use of incentives has been repeatedly recommended in management literature, I wish to emphasize an additional need to build into the education and training program an ideological and humanistic base for development. People involved in development projects—in whatever capacity and regardless of their level in the administrative hierarchy—should feel that they are not just filling jobs for earning a living, they are functioning in essential roles for improving the quality of human life. Dedication to serve human goals in the present era of national development is vitally important and should be encouraged as part of the political socialization process. Also, relevant to a proper functioning of resettlement administration is the idea of continuity. It is imperative, I think, that governments keep the resettlement administrative agencies operating until at least the transitional period is over. Dissolving them right after the completion of the community's physical displacement would result in increased stress and prompt an insecure feeling among the relocatees. Conceiving resettlement as a longitudinal process would require the continuity of the same administration for monitoring events, periodic assessment of the situation, and acting as a liaison agency between the relocatees and the various government departments.

These responsibilities, however, ought to be gradually handed over to settlers' organizations, local government councils, and ministerial departments operational at the local level. Since neither a rapid nor slow devolution of responsibilities would be good for the resettlement scheme, the best compromise, as Scudder proposes, would be that, "in preparation for a timely transfer, the centralized settlement authorities encourage from the very beginning the development of a carefully selected number of settler organizations and the development and utilization of certain local government capabilities" (1980:9).

People and Decision-making. Related to the organizational aspect of resettlement and development is the dilemma of people's participation. It is a dilemma because participation is strongly recommended by many, but no agreement has been reached on the form or the extent of people's roles in projects that affect their lives. In viewing social management aspects as a source of trouble for most irrigation projects, Nelson and Tileston, for example, suggest that "if the activity is to be successful, the cultivators must be involved more intimately in all management and operation aspects, particularly in those elements of the system that directly impinge upon or affect their holdings" (1977:23). Contrary to this view, however, several participants in the 1971 Cairo workshop, some of whom were government officials, thought that the role of settlers should be advisory and not that of decision-making. Others, including myself, wished to see the relocatees involved in the decision-making process as well, but this is a debatable matter where the issues are related to domestic politics, cultural norms and values, individual capabilities and desires.

Nonetheless, I view as important the differentiation between ceremonial versus substantial participation. To cite only one example, taking a group of Nubian representatives to show them a house model and listen with concern to their remarks was a ceremonial participation, whereas if Nubians had been consulted prior to designing the new houses and if the final plan would have accommodated both the architectural rationale and the traditional concerns, this would have been a substantial participation. Women also should have been consulted. A house model can mean nothing without its context. Perhaps one way to experiment on a minute scale and assess people's reaction and suggestions would be through the creation of a new village as a pilot project long before the actual move of the entire population.

I also wish to differentiate here between "early" versus "late" participation. In effect, I can assume that the more substantial people's participation becomes and the earlier it has an input in the planning process of resettlement, the more likely that stress upon relocation could be reduced. Progress toward adjustment would also become possible at an early stage following displacement. Resettlement planners should work with the relocatees not just plan for them. They also should set, as an ultimate goal, to turn management over to the relocatees in the shortest possible time following effective orientation and training. I realize that this is a difficult task. Nonetheless, it becomes possible through serious and adequate utilization of relevant social-science research findings.

Data Base. Resettlement management needs, of course, adequate information to draw upon and to act accordingly. Such information has always been conceived mostly in terms of surveys that usually provide figures, percentages, and tabular information on the physical and human resources of the displaced community, whether prior to or after relocation. Should systematic sociocultural research be requested, its input has usually been either too late or too little to have any effect on planning decisions. Nubian resettlement is a case in point.

Planners and administrators frequently repeat the mistakes that have been made in the past because they do not take into account the relocatees' coping strategies and certain key problem areas regarding a settlement's relationship with its habitat, both of which have important policy implications. Because of this unfortunate phenomenon, greater efforts should be made to present the results of research to planners at an appropriate time and in an appropriate fashion. Both Scudder and I argue "that while we do not suspect the planners' intelligence and consciousness, we urge the need for an educational approach on land settlement issues and national development problems in general. The World Bank has recently made a good start along this line in terms of organizing in-service seminars and issuing periodic guidelines, papers and memoranda. At the national level, concerned government departments, in collaboration with research institutions, should get involved in an educational endeavor for both planners and researchers in an attempt to bridge the gap, increase communication and enhance possibilities for success in development efforts" (Fahim and Scudder 1981:202).

Concluding Remarks

Despite documented financial, ecological, and human costs associated with the formation of large-scale man-made lakes, the construction of dams will continue; and consequently more populations will be displaced. Dams have always been justified in terms of their development potentialities, and dam-related population resettlement schemes have been viewed as an opportunity to induce rapid socioeconomic change among the affected groups through the intensification of agriculture at the new sites and the provision of education, health care, and other community services. Nevertheless, resettlement has proved to be a difficult and complex operation, as is apparent in the Nubian case. Adjustment to relocation and settlement in a new habitat are also painstaking and involve a multidimensional and longitudinal process. In commenting on the African resettlement schemes, Thayer Scudder is correct that "it is hard to imagine a more dramatic way to illustrate impotence than to forcibly eject people from a preferred habitat against their will" (1973:51).

Although adjustment to resettlement can be facilitated and accelerated by introducing viable development means, the Nubian case clearly showed that this is not an easy task. Because the implementation of resettlement was rushed in order to meet the deadlines set by the engineering work at the dam site, both Nubians and resettlement administrators suffered from the agony of moving people to an area that was not yet ready to accommodate them adequately. Although both the relocatees and the resettlement administration tried hard to cope with such an unfavorable situation, it soon became evident that some important errors had been made in planning and implementing resettlement. The problems of 1980 can find their roots in the very early stage of the Nubian resettlement scheme.

This study of Nubian resettlement in Egypt has shown that the planning of the physical layout of the new villages and the distribution of houses and services has been largely shortsighted in terms of future expansion of the community. Planners seem to have overlooked the possibility that significant numbers of additional people would pour into the area and incorporate themselves into resident groups. Unless there are corrective measures taken, the demographic, social, and health consequences of relatively overcrowded villages and living quarters, aggravated by inadequate services and insufficient economic opportunities, will definitely be an increase in the flow of people out of the new community.

Nonetheless, these remarks should not lead to the belief that the displacement of the Nubian community in Egypt resulted only in stressful conditions and contributed no positive aspects at all. It is an established fact that resettlement caused stress to Nubians, but it has also had its good aspects which Nubians themselves, on occasion, admit and appreciate. Some immediate and obvious results have been the steady decline in infant mortality despite a substantial increase during the first two years following relocation and the provision of adequate health care for the entire community in addition to a presumably better nutritional standard than Nubians ever had access to in the old region. Equally important is the availability of education and work opportunities for both men and women.

Resettlement seems to have brought the Nubians' basic needs to the attention of the government and it also introduced them to the nation as a group with a potentially influential role to play in the country's serious attempts to bring about socioeconomic development, especially in the Aswan region. Furthermore, resettlement ended the long-established isolation of the Nubian community from the rest of the country and their deprivation from adequate and necessary services and rights. It brought them, once and for all, to modern life with all its conveniences and troubles.

Chapter Eleven
Research Notes and Reflections

*Look and think before opening the shutter. The heart and mind
are the true lens of the camera.*

Yousuf Karsh, a Canadian photographer

AT THE OUTSET

My association with the Nubians began in 1963 as a research
assistant in the Social Research Center of the American University in
Cairo. From 1963 to 1964 I was involved with a study of cultural
change in a previously resettled Nubian village in the Kom Ombo
area. During the two years following this original study, I was able
to observe the relocation process at Kom Ombo and collect material
for my Ph.D. dissertation on the Nubian resettlement (1968).

After obtaining my degree, I returned to Egypt in October 1968,
and once again resumed my research among the Nubians by conduct-
ing a follow-up study in the winter of 1969. My concern at that time
was to establish academic credibility for myself, and I approached my
research as a "typical" anthropologist by studying aspects of culture
change among the Nubians as a result of relocation. Later, that same
summer, I carried out a two-month field study among the resettled
Nubians in their new land for the purpose of developing a comparative framework between the Egyptian and Sudanese experiences in
resettling. Although this approach was academically exciting and
useful in helping me gain insights into the adaptation processes of the
Nubians, it did not give me satisfaction in terms of serving people.
I soon felt out of place and at a distance from the reality I was trying

173

to understand. Unable to serve, I felt of little value to the people I was studying, and what disturbed me the most was the constant anguish and struggle of the people in the midst of a series of surveys and studies that seemed to offer no solutions or immediate relief for their problems.

While knowledge of a situation may be of interest and importance, without constructive action it may prove futile; and I was beginning to realize that the studies in themselves were limiting. Then, in 1971, I became the principal investigator of a research project on the evaluation of the resettlement scheme sponsored by the Social Research Center at the American University in Cairo in collaboration with a government department, the Egyptian Organization for Land Cultivation and Development. The study was financially sponsored by the U.S. Department of Health, Education and Welfare. This study was soon disrupted because Egypt was then in a state of war with Israel, and the research site became part of a sensitive military zone. As a result, the research team was instructed on several occasions to cut short its presence in the area and, sometimes, to pack and leave. In a two-year period, however, the research team paid several visits to the resettlement area and investigated the resettlement problems with the administrators and the Nubian leaders.

A Decade Later

In the summer of 1973, after nearly a decade since my original involvement with the Nubian research, I paid a second visit to Khashm el-Girba, visiting with the resettled Sudanese Nubians and following up on recent developments. In the fall of 1973, I was granted a fellowship by the Ford Foundation and left for the United States for one academic year in residence at the California Institute of Technology (CALTECH) in Pasadena. My choosing CALTECH was due to my desire to work closely with Professor Thayer Scudder, who had done research among the Nubians prior to their relocation and had also carried out intensive studies on various dam-related resettlement schemes in Africa. Moreover, he was then engaged in developing a resettlement theory of how people respond to relocation and how this affects the design and implementation of development programs on the new site. My recollection of the CALTECH period is that my accomplishment was very limited and hardly inspiring as I went through a state of psychological depression caused by dissatisfaction and anger over the state of political affairs in my home country. I was particularly worried about the aftermath of the Middle East war in which immediate family members participated.

In Pasadena, I always wondered about the relevance of my research work to the Nubians, to the country, and even to my personal life and professional career. I also questioned whether it would be worthwhile to devote much time in directing my research goal to the development of a "theory," be it on resettlement or any other human activity. What should take priority in the professional training and practice of non-Western anthropologists, given the fact that emphasis in their home countries is placed on the process of change rather than theorizing about it? Furthermore, is it appropriate for me to confine myself to the microcosmic approach that anthropology has traditionally emphasized, and consequently feel cutoff from national concerns and problems? These questions and others preoccupied my thinking and stimulated a serious and harsh self-inquiry about the role of social scientists in a world that was then, and still is, beset with drastic human problems that concern and affect all people in all countries. The outcome of that intellectual conflict was a decision to return home and explore ways in which I could be useful to my country, or at least help the Nubians cope with the resettlement hardships.

When I returned to my home base in May 1974, I was asked to resume the Nubian study, which had been interrupted. A research team was formed and upon the request of the sponsoring government department an interview schedule was constructed to investigate specific questions related mainly to the agricultural policies and practices. A preliminary household survey was done on the basis of a small sample, but the survey data proved to be useless and unreliable due to false information provided by the interviewees. The Nubians not only showed a lack of interest, and sometimes resented being asked for information, but also expressed their antagonism toward our presence. In some instances it became difficult to pursue research. These attitudes were intensified by the presence of several researchers from government departments and universities; this caused a Nubian to note that "the difference between Old and New Nubia is that the former has been innundated by distructive water while the latter has been flooded by useless research." The Social Research Center studies were finally halted in winter of 1974, and the result was a period of anguish and disappointment.

I should say here that the Nubians also had expressed an apprehension about the outcome of research. This not only attests to their sense of cultural pride, it also reflects their need for something tangible that would tell the story of migration and preserve their cultural heritage. Delay in the publication of materials, especially those gathered by non-Western researchers who conducted their studies in the first half of the sixties, and the eventual appearance of publications only in the English language had begun to create unfavorable sentiments.

Although Fernea and Gerster's illustrated book (1973) on the Nubians, which appeared thirteen years after the ethnological survey began, was well received, the Nubians expressed a desire to have a publication that they could read, respond to, and make use of. This led me to present a series of short articles on my research findings in a Nubian bi-monthly magazine, although the number of essays was limited due to my leaving Egypt in the latter part of 1973 on a post-doctoral fellowship at the California Institute of Technology. These articles, printed in simple language, were intended to provide basic information on the Nubian communities, introducing the reader to the importance of research and its significance in daily life.

As an outgrowth of this experience I was able to perceive that people subjected to anthropological research have a right to see research through to its conclusion. Such publications in the local language could then serve as a useful tool in the development of indigenous anthropology, providing a more concise portrayal of the ongoing cultural changes so that people might reflect on and identify with the cultural patterns of behavior that continually shape their future. Not only would such publications serve as a social history, they would serve as evidence that people do not easily give up a culture but, instead, use it in their attempt to create solutions to conflict situations.

Although the Nubian study had a formal affiliation with the concerned government departments, in terms of granting the research permit and facilitating fieldwork, the research findings had no impact on policy. Among the reasons for this nonutilization of research results are those related to shifts in policies and the turnover of government officials and administrators. While the Social Research Center had formal recognition and government support for its undertaking, it had never become involved, even in an advisory capacity, in the policy-making process in connection with the Nubian resettlement problems.

At times I felt that the talk of research input for development was no more than ostentatious lip service without a serious intention to utilize the findings in the policy-making process so that strengths could be capitalized on and weaknesses corrected.

In searching for an explanation of research nonutilization, Maday attributes it to "ignorance of the substance and applicability of the existing knowledge and to the lack of communication between the anthropological profession (or social sciences) and society at large" (1975:6). In my view, however, the core of the problem lies in the lack of political support for social-science knowledge having a deter-mining input in forming the destiny of man. Political considerations, I discovered, very often override the wisdom of scientific minds. Unfortunately, research findings, like conference recommendations, quite often reach a dead end or, as Qadeer precisely said, "bring forth a feeling of emptiness' (1977:13).

Reflecting on this period, I recognize that the position of principal investigator in a policy-oriented research assignment gave me greater access to official records and information, expanding my knowledge of Egypt's goals regarding resettlement and leading to a better under-standing of the administration's logistics and rationales. This under-standing broadened my analytical perspective and allowed me to see both sides of the resettlement issue. Prior to this, I had continued to share the feelings of many of the researchers and anthropologists regarding resettlement of the Nubians. These feelings of deep sympathy and distress at seeing a culture uprooted were common among most foreign researchers during the 1960–64 Nubian ethnological survey, and it was only as I began to see the advantages the resettled Nubians had in comparison with neighboring groups that I began to appreciate the effort and monetary cost incurred in meeting the Nubians' needs at a time when Egypt was beset with substantial financial problems. This resulted in my becoming more empathic with both the adminis-tration's and the Nubians' problems. Also, being aware of the adminis-tration's attempts to accommodate the Nubians, I was not entirely favorable toward certain situations that arose involving exaggerated demands and definite exploitation of the administration by specific groups of Nubians.

NEW INSIGHTS AND DIRECTIONS

During the period from 1975 to 1980, I was exposed to situations and became involved in activities that resulted in a concrete change in my research perspectives and role as an anthropologist. In 1975, I attended a Wenner-Gren Foundation symposium at Burg Wartenstein, Austria, on "Long-Term Field Research in Social Anthropology," and learned a great deal about the methodology of longitudinal studies and was able to identify serious methodological shortcomings in my Nubian study and gain insights that are outlined later in this chapter. Again in 1978, I returned to Burg Wartenstein for another Wenner-Gren symposium on "Indigenous Anthropology in Non-Western Countries," which profoundly educated me on how to deal with and relate to research problems pertinent to a foreign/indigenous perspective in applied anthropology that I had explored in an earlier paper (Fahim 1977). In addition to these two intellectual and academic events, since 1975 I have participated on several occasions in consultancy work on different resettlement schemes in West Africa and the Middle East. This practical experience taught me the need for and the value of a resettlement theory for policy implications; it also showed me that my research experience and findings among the Nubians could be utilized elsewhere. Last but not least came a new phase of encounter with the Nubians in 1976, when I worked for the National Academy of Scientific Research and Technology in Egypt as a coordinator of research projects dealing with the socioeconomic impacts of the Aswan High Dam and related projects. This assignment brought me back to the Nubians but in a different context and in a different role as the following discussion points out.

These professional experiences prompt me to suggest that the anthropologist's role is one of constant change, and it is essential for the researcher to identify the factors directly affecting such transformations. The first factor fundamentally involves the anthropologist's perspective since—in spite of the fact that anthropologists, whether indigenous or foreign, presumably share the same research training and its professional goals—the indigenous anthropologist is understandably more compatible with the situation, and this would undoubtedly affect his orientation in the practice of anthropology. While this position may be advantageous in some respects, keeping an objective viewpoint is essential, and this may be best achieved by collaboration with not only national and local groups but also with foreign researchers (Fahim and Helmer 1980). The issue, however, "is not how we can keep out intrusive values by virtue of the problems we study and the methods we use but how we can take systematic accounts of the values and subjective considerations that inevitably enter into our research" (Kelman 1968:5).

This brings us to the relationship between the local anthropologist and the state when national projects are involved. Although resettlement necessarily implies uprooting established cultures—something social scientists in general dislike to see happen—the anthropologist needs to perceive large-scale technological projects as regional or national phenomena rather than strictly as local community matters. I wish to take issue here, in particular, with a tendency among certain Western intellectual camps to denounce the collaboration of Third World social scientists with government agencies for the purpose of integrating groups such as the Nubians into the national context. Furthermore, anthropologists must reconsider the widespread idea that massive change is inherently destructive, requiring them to emphasize only the harmful effects of large-scale projects. Instead, the need to reflect both the positive and negative aspects of relocation is essential in order to avoid a biased approach to similar problems in other situations regarding extensive relocation. The offensive, anti-state attitude advocated by quite a few contemporary anthropologists, largely from the West, which assumes that the government is attempting to incorporate minorities into the national scheme for the purpose of exploiting them and their resources, must be dealt with in a more realistic way. This is particularly necessary in an assessment of Third World countries, which desperately need to utilize their natural resources (Fahim 1977).

METHODOLOGICAL ISSUES

Despite my residence in the United States since 1975, my work for the Egyptian National Academy and consultancy for international development agencies (e.g., the Agency for International Aid, the Canadian Agency for International Development) allowed me to go to Egypt frequently and thus visit with the Nubians. During these visits, I met with as many Nubians as possible to present and discuss the findings of my study. This was arranged through several meetings at the Nubian clubs in Cairo and Alexandria, involving small groups from seven to twenty participants each time. These meetings drew both the young and the old from the cities of Cairo and Alexandria as well as those from New Nubia who happened to be visiting.

By becoming actively involved with the Nubians through these discussions, I regained a sense of integrity regarding my professional commitments and began to see that such research is of great value regardless of the frustrations, pitfalls, and shortcomings I had previously experienced. I also began to realize the importance of developing a relocation theory out of observing and studying the resettlement process over a span of time. I was particularly intrigued by the potential policy implications of such a theory. As a result I became more concerned with synthesizing my own conceptual framework on human resettlement, which proved to be extremely useful in appraisal missions for the World Bank in connection with some resettlement schemes in West Africa.

In longitudinal studies, in which the researcher follows the same population or phenomenon over time, several professional and personal problems begin to emerge. On the professional level, my long-term involvement with the study of Nubian resettlement in Egypt and the follow-up on the Sudanese case, have made apparent several major methodological issues that distinguish this type of research from the usual one-shot study in the field of anthropology. In longitudinal resettlement research, I share the view with both Scudder and Colson, who wrote that "anthropologists are studying dynamic sets of interrelationships that are highly responsive to the context in which they occur" (1979:241). Knowledge of the chronological order of events and data collecting are important, but so are the relative values of the events and the need to inform the people and professionals so as to prevent a repetition of mistakes. This eventual realization gave me the impetus to review my material and write a manuscript that might prove useful to other resettlement schemes.

The methodology of comparisons between life before and after relocation (commonly used in one-shot studies) seems to me insufficient because it fails to trace and interpret the mechanisms that people develop to cope with relocation. Scudder and Colson found that people frequently "experiment, test the gains and losses, and decide whether it is worth pursuing a new course" (1979:241). Consequently, there is a pressing need to investigate and assess resettlement projects as part of an ongoing process, not only by evaluating the traditional behavioral patterns of each particular group but also by considering external factors at the macro level, including interaction with the host group and the scheme's administrators. In this respect, Scudder and Colson state: "We are not dealing with systems that move mechanistically toward adaptive states. On the contrary, we are dealing with people making decisions through time in contexts which change both because of their own actions and because of changes in external conditions which often neither they nor we are able to anticipate" (1979:241). This approach will allow the study of how the displaced community adapts to the new settings; and, probably more significantly, in terms of theory and policy it will investigate the relocatee's response to relocation.

Resettlement has forced the Nubians into new modes of communication, directly affecting their nature and expanding their abilities and hopes for the future. These new methods of interaction and the constantly changing values must be assessed along with the cultural variables in order to predict the future with any certainty. In the past, anthropologists have traditionally tended to observe the cultural constants; but our roles must now reflect the changes we are studying, especially those performed by local anthropologists, who, in many cases, are personally affected by these changes.

Another important methodological issue relates to the fact that data accumulates in long-term research as a result of repeated visits; and unless it is coded, analyzed, and written up, the researcher may later find it difficult to put the data in a chronological sequence. For instance, because of my frequent relocations and travels, it has been difficult for me to keep my records in order. Anthropologists involved in long-term studies also seem to face a common dilemma in how best to deal with data in a time frame. Scudder and Colson concluded that probably the best approach to longitudinal research in social anthropology is through collecting data on small samples (1979:249). Discussing this point with me, Scudder argued that in following these samples, the researcher can easily and accurately gain insights into problems of importance to administrators and scholars alike. The use of a small sample that the researcher can examine periodically seems to be an appropriate methodological strategy because it allows the investigation of certain questions at the micro level, which must be explored before a general assessment of the situation can be made. For instance, to examine economic viability, the researcher can—through such samples—obtain rather detailed and accurate information on how much income a displaced Nubian family with a modally sized farm makes, what such a family's expenses are, and the amount of income received from other job opportunities. It would have been extremely beneficial to me in undertaking a longitudinal study among the displaced Nubians had this approach been part of my earlier methodological orientation.

I again come to the category of problems that relate specifically to the researcher. In long-term studies, as years go by, anthropologists age as do their informants and friends in the community under study. How much of that early excitement of fieldwork and enthusiasm of discovery do we researchers maintain over time? Personally and professionally, researchers change over time and so do their study people or communities. How would this affect research objectives in the long run, the process and results, as change in substance may lead to change in form? I believe, therefore, that a change affecting either the researcher or the community may, at a certain point, require both a temporary halt to the investigations and a fresh input from others. These questions and issues were raised and discussed extensively during the 1975 Wenner-Gren symposium on long-term anthropological research as well as in its proceedings (Foster et al. 1979).

FUTURE RESEARCH IN NUBIA

I encourage now more than ever continued research on the Nubian case; but it has to be systematic, coordinated, and of potential service to the people. Anthropologists can render invaluable assistance to the Nubians in two areas. Given the existing knowledge of the Nubian culture and the research findings of adjustment problems in Kom Ombo, researchers may be able to help both the Nubians and the government in planning new settlements along the lake's shores. Several groups of Nubians actually moved on their own initiative to the lake area and built homesteads. Another service that can be offered to the Nubians relates to the present efforts to compile information and collect artifacts that would preserve their cultural heritage.

I perceive, at this point, an urgent need for a dialogue among those, both foreign and national, who participated in Nubian studies before and after relocation and who represent the different subfields or research areas of the discipline of anthropology. While there is an International Society for Nubian Studies that meets once every three or four years and discusses Nubian archaeological issues, there should also be some means for integrating the diverse and substantial anthropological contributions toward a comprehensive ethnological study and understanding of a single culture and people. This would also render a considerable service to the Nubians, for, as Appell rightly says, "if a people have access to their cultural traditions and are able to evaluate them positively, they have the resources to cope creatively with the social change and move into the future without apprehension" (1977:475).

In conclusion to this chapter, I wish to say that my research experience among the Nubians, although uneasy and frustrating at times, has been extremely rewarding both personally and professionally. I now have greater faith in people and a greater desire to serve them. I learned that people are indeed resourceful if challenged. They are amazingly capable, under difficult circumstances, to think properly, act effectively, and innovate creatively.

The issue that now occupies my mind is how we, as social scientists involved in the change process in our own countries, can act to assist not only the affected people but also those who plan and implement in accomplishing their ultimate human tasks. We, as researchers, may be able to best identify the cultural, administrative, and political potentialities or constraints; but this knowledge must be used for the people's welfare because knowledge without humanistic application leads nowhere. There can be no lasting development without the ingredients of human dignity and constructive progress. It is in serving people that we help them achieve human goals as we fulfill our role as committed and humane social scientists.

References

Abdel Wahab, Fikri
    1964   Some resettlement problems. Paper presented at a symposium on contemporary Egyptian Nubia, Aswan, Egypt.

Ackermann, William C., Gilbert F. White, and E. B. Worthington, eds.
    1973   *Man-made lakes: Their problems and environmental effects.* Geophysical Monograph 17. Washington, D.C.: American Geophysical Union.

Adams, William Y.
    1977   *Nubia: Corridor to Africa.* Princeton: Princeton University Press.

Agouba, I. Mukhtar
    1980   Social change in rural Sudanese communities: A Case study of an agricultural development scheme in the Sudan (Khashm el-Girba). Ph.D. dissertation, University of Khartoum.

Appell, G. N.
    1977   The Blight of indigenous peoples: Issues and dilemmas. *Survival International Review* 3:11–16.

Barbour, Kenneth M.
    1961   *The Republic of the Sudan: A Regional geography.* London: University of London Press.

Bryant, J. H.
    1980   Foreword in *Uprooting and development: Dilemmas of coping with modernization,* ed. George V. Coelho and Paul I. Ahmed. New York and London: Plenum Press.

Butcher, D. A. P.
    1971   *An Organizational manual for resettlement: A Systematic approach to the resettlement problem created by man-made lakes, with special reference for West Africa.* Rome: Food and Agriculture Organization of the United Nations.

Chambers, Robert
    1969   *Settlement schemes in tropical Africa: A Study of organizations and development.* New York: Praeger Publishers.

185

Coelho, George V., and Paul I. Ahmed, eds.
  1980   *Uprooting and development: Dilemmas of coping with modernization.* New York and London: Plenum Press.

Colson, Elizabeth
  1971   *The Social consequences of resettlement: The Impact of the Kariba resettlement upon the Gwembe Tonga.* Manchester: Manchester University Press.

Dafalla, Hassan
  1975   *The Nubian exodus.* London: C. Hurst and Co.

Dinesen, Isak (pseud.)
  1972   *Out of Africa.* New York: Vintage Books.

Driver, Ely, and Walter Wunderlich, eds.
  1979   *Environmental effects of hydraulic engineering works.* Proceedings of an International Symposium in Knoxville, Tennessee, 1978. Knoxville: Tennessee Valley Authority.

Emery, Walter B.
  1965   *Egypt in Nubia.* London: Hutchinson.

Fahim, Hussein M.
  1968   The Resettlement of Egyptian Nubians: A Case study in developmental change. Ph.D. dissertation, University of California, Berkeley.
  1973   Nubian resettlement in the Sudan. *Ekistics* 36(212):42–49.
  1977   Foreign and indigenous anthropology: The Perspectives of an Egyptian anthropologist. *Human Organization* 36(1):80–86.
  1979a Community health aspects of Nubian resettlement in Egypt. In *From Tzintzuntzan to the "image of limited good": Essays in the honor of George M. Foster,* ed. Margaret Clark, Robert V. Kemper, and Cynthia Nelson. Kroeber Anthropological Society, Papers 55–56. Berkeley: The Society.
  1979b Field research in a Nubian village: The Experience of an Egyptian anthropologist. In *Long-term field research in social anthropology,* ed. George M. Foster et al. New York: Academic Press.
  1980   Nubian resettlement and nomadic sedentarization in Khashm el-Girba scheme, eastern Sudan. In *When nomads settle: Processes of sedentarization as adaptation and response,* ed. Philip C. Salzman. New York: Praeger Publishers.
  1981   *Dams, people, and development: The Aswan High Dam case.* New York: Pergamon Press.

Fahim, Hussein M., and Katherine Helmer
  1980   Further remarks on indigenous anthropology in non-western countries. *Current Anthropology* 21:644–50.

Fahim, Hussein M., and Thayer Scudder
  1981   *The development potential of land settlement: The Egyptian case.* Proceedings of an International Symposium on Social Research for Development. Cairo Papers, vol. 4, Monographs 2 and 3. Cairo: The American University in Cairo.

Fahim, Hussein M., W. Vogt, and M. Mickle
  1979 The modeling of community relocation and relocation processes. *In* Proceedings of a Conference on Simulation and Modeling, University of Pittsburgh, 1977.

Fatehi, Hassan
  1966 Notes on Nubian architecture. In *Contemporary Egyptian Nubia*, vol. 1, ed. Robert A. Fernea. New Haven: Human Relations Area Files.

Fernea, Robert A.
  1962 The Use of pilot communities as an approach to Nubian resettlement. Report presented to the Ministry of Social Affairs and Agencies concerned with Nubian resettlement, Cairo, Egypt.
  1966 Introduction to *Contemporary Egyptian Nubia*, vol. 1, ed. Robert A. Fernea. New Haven: Human Relations Area Files.
  1979 Administration of resettlement schemes. In *Human settlements on new lands: Their design and development*, ed. Laila El Hamamsy and Jeannie Garrison. Proceedings of a workshop in Alexandria, Egypt, 1971. Cairo: The American University in Cairo Press.

Fernea Robert A., and Georg Gerster
  1973 *Nubians in Egypt: Peaceful people.* Austin and London: University of Texas Press.

Fernea, Robert A., and John G. Kennedy
  1966 Initial adaptations to resettlement: A New life for Egyptian Nubians. *Current Anthropology* 7:349–54.

Foster, George M.
  1979 Community building: A Rapporteur's statement. In *Human settlements on new lands: Their design and development*, ed. Laila El Hamamsy and Jeannie Garrison. Proceedings of a workshop in Alexandria, Egypt, 1971. Cairo: The American University in Cairo Press.

Foster, George, et al., eds.
  1979 *Long-term field research in social anthropology.* New York: Academic Press.

Fried, Marc
  1963 Grieving for a lost home. In *Urban conditions: People and policy in the metropolis*, ed. Leonard J. Duhl. New York: Basic Books.

Gauvain, Mary, Irwin Altman, and Hussein M. Fahim
  1983 Homes and social change: A Cross-cultural analysis. In *Environmental psychology: Directions and perspectives,* ed. N. Feimer and S. Geller (forthcoming). New York: Praeger Publishers.

Geiser, Peter
  1966 Some impressions concerning the nature and extent of stabilization and urbanization in Nubian society. In *Contemporary Egyptian Nubia*, vol. 1, ed. Robert A. Fernea. New Haven: Human Relations Area Files.
  1967 Some differential factors affecting population movement: The Nubian case. *Human Organization* 26(3):164–77.
  1973 The Myth of the dam. *American Anthropologist* 75:184–94.

Gerster, Georg
    1963   Threatened treasures of the Nile. *National Geographic Magazine*
            124:587–621.

Gouldner, Alvin
    1964   Anti-Minotaur: The Myth of a value-free sociology. In *The New
            sociology: Essays in social science and social theory in honor of
            C. Wright Mills*, ed. Irving L. Horowitz. New York: Oxford Uni-
            versity Press.

Greener, Leslie
    1962   *High dam over Nubia*. London: Cassell and Co.

Hale, Sondra
    1979   The Changing ethnic identity of Nubians in an urban milieu: Khar-
            toum, Sudan. Ph.D. dissertation, University of California, Los Angeles.

El Hamamsy, Laila
    1979   Introduction to *Human settlements on new lands: Their design and
            development*, ed. Laila El Hamamsy and Jeannie Garrison. Proceed-
            ings of a workshop in Alexandria, Egypt, 1971. Cairo: The American
            University in Cairo Press.

El Hamamsy, Laila, and Jeannie Garrison, eds.
    1979   *Human settlements on new lands: Their design and development*.
            Proceedings of a workshop in Alexandria, Egypt, 1971. Cairo: The
            American University in Cairo Press.

Hansen, Art, and Anthony Oliver-Smith, eds.
    1982   *Involuntary migration and resettlement: The Problems and responses
            of dislocated peoples*. Boulder: Westview Press.

Heikal, Bahiga
    1966   Residence patterns in Ismailia, Ballana. In *Contemporary Egyptian
            Nubia*, vol. 2, ed. Robert A. Fernea. New Haven: Human Relations
            Area Files.

Heikal, Mohamed Hassanein
    1973   *The Cairo documents: The Inside story of Nasser and his relationship
            with world leaders, rebels, and statesmen*. Garden City: Doubleday.

Helmer, Katherine
    1979   Nubians in London: A Report on preliminary fieldwork. Photocopy.

Hohenwart, Anna
    1963   Research in Egyptian Nubia. *International Committee on Urgent
            Anthropological and Ethnological Research, Bulletin* 6:25–29.
    1975   *Reflections on the Nubian society: A Memorial volume for P. C.
            Laufer Herder*. West Germany: F. Reiburg/Breisgau.
    1979   *Nubien forschungen*. Series Africana 14. Vienna: Eigentümer, Ver-
            leger and Druck.

Honigman, John
    1976   The personal approach in cultural anthropological research. *Current
            Anthropology* 17:243–61.

Horton, Alan W.
    1964 *The Egyptian Nubians: Some information on their ethnography and resettlement.* American Universities Field Staff Reports Service, Northeast Africa Series, vol. 11, issue 2.

International Bank for Reconstruction and Development. *See* World Bank.

Jansson, Kurt
    1979 The planning of new land settlements in terms of social goals. In *Human settlements on new lands: Their design and development,* ed. Laila El Hamamsy and Jeannie Garrison. Proceedings of a workshop in Alexandria, Egypt, 1971. Cairo: The American University in Cairo Press.

Keating, Rex
    1978 *Nubian rescue.* New York: Harcourt, Brace and World.

Kelman, Herbert C.
    1968 *A Time to speak: On human values and social research.* San Francisco: Jossey-Bass.

Kennedy, John G.
    1970 Aman Doger, Nubian monster of the Nile. *Journal of American Folklore* 83:438–45.
    1977 *Struggle for change in a Nubian community.* Palo Alto: Mayfield Publishing Co.
(ed.)
    1978 *Nubian ceremonial life: Studies in Islamic syncretism and cultural change.* Berkeley and Cairo: The American University in Cairo Press.

Kronenberg, A., and W. Kronenberg
    1963 Preliminary report on anthropological field work in Sudanese Nubia, 1961–1962. *Kush* 11:302–11.
    1964 Preliminary report on anthropological field work in Sudanese Nubia, 1962–1963. *Kush* 12:282–90.
    1965a Preliminary report on the anthropological field work in Sudanese Nubia, 1963–1964. *Kush* 13:205–12.
    1965b Parallel cousin: Marriage in medieval and modern Nubia. *Kush* 13:241–60.

Lagler, Karl F., ed.
    1969 *Man-made lakes: Planning and development.* Rome: Food and Agriculture Organization of the United Nations.

Maday, Bela C., ed.
    1975 Introduction to *Anthropology and Society.* Washington, D.C.: Anthropological Society of Washington.

Nelson, Gary, and Fred Tileston
    1977 Why irrigation projects may become enduring monuments to failure. *International Development Review* 19(3):22–24.

Palmer, Gary
    1974 The Ecology of resettlement schemes. *Human Organization* 33(3): 239–50.

Qadeer, Mohammad A.
   1977   The Futility of world conferences. *International Development Review*
          19(1):13–15.

Reusch, Jurgen, Annemarie Jacobson, and Martin B. Loeb
   1948   Acculturation and illness. *Psychological Monographs, General and
          Applied* 62 (5), (whole no. 292).

Scaff, Alvin
   1961/62 Report on the Wadi Halfa resettlement to the United Nations Eco-
          nomic Commission for Africa. Photocopy.

Scudder, Thayer
   1966   The Economic basis of Egyptian Nubian labour migration. In *Con-
          temporary Egyptian Nubia*, vol. 1, ed. Robert A. Fernea. New Haven:
          Human Relations Area Files.
   1973   *The Human ecology of big projects: River basin development and
          resettlement.* Annual Review of Anthropology, vol. 2. Palo Alto:
          Annual Review.
   1975   Resettlement. In *Man-made lakes and human health*, ed. Neville F.
          Stanley and Michael P. Alpers. London and New York: Academic
          Press.
   1976   Social impacts of integrated river basin development on local popula-
          tion. In *River Basin Development: Policies and planning*, vol. 1. Pro-
          ceedings of the United Nations Interregional Seminar on River Basin
          and Interbasin Development in Budapest, Hungary, 1975. New York:
          United Nations.
   1979   The Development potential of agricultural settlement in new lands.
          Research proposal submitted to the Agency for International Develop-
          ment, Washington, D.C. Photocopy.
   1980   The Development potential of agricultural settlement in new lands.
          A second 6-month progress report for the Agency for International
          Development, Washington, D.C. Photocopy.
   1981   What it means to be dammed: The Anthropology of large-scale devel-
          opment projects in the tropics and subtropics. *Engineering and Sci-
          ence* 64(4):9–15.

Scudder, Thayer, and Elizabeth Colson
   1979   Long-term research in Gwembe Valley, Zambia. In *Long-term field
          research in social anthropology*, ed. George M. Foster et al. New
          York: Academic Press.
   1982   From welfare to development: A Conceptual framework for the
          analysis of dislocated people. In *Involuntary immigration and reset-
          tlement: The Problems and responses of dislocated peoples*, ed. Art
          Hansen and Anthony Oliver-Smith. Boulder: Westview Press.

Smelser, Neil J.
   1968   *Essays in sociological explanation.* Englewood Cliffs, N.J.: Prentice-
          Hall.

Smock, David
   1967   The Role of anthropology in a western Nigerian resettlement project.
          In *The Anthropology of development in Sub-Saharah Africa*, ed.

David Brokensha and Marion Peersall. Society for Applied Anthropology, Monograph 10. Lexington, Ky.: The Society.

Sörbö, Gunnar
  1977a Nomads on the scheme: A Study of irrigation agriculture and pastoralism in eastern Sudan. In *Land use and development*, ed. Phil O'Keefe and Ben Wisner. London: International African Institute.
  1977b *How to survive development: The Story of New Halfa*. Development Studies and Research Center, Monograph Series 6. Khartoum: University of Khartoum.
  1980   Off-scheme interests and economic differentiation in Sudanese tenant communities. Paper presented to the World Bank, Washington, D.C. Photocopy.

Stanley, Neville F., and Michael P. Alpers, eds.
  1975 *Man-made lakes and human health*. London and New York: Academic Press.

Sterling, Clair
  1972 The Aswan disaster. In *Our chemical environment*, ed. John C. Giddings and Manus B. Monroe. Scranton, Penn.: Canfield Press.

Tadros, Helmi
  1980 Factors obstructing community development in Egypt's reclaimed lands. Paper presented at the Fifth World Congress for Rural Sociology, Mexico City, Mexico.

Trimble, Joseph E.
  1980 Forced migration: Its impact on shaping coping strategies. In *Uprooting and development: Dilemmas of coping with modernization*, ed. George V. Coelho and Paul I. Ahmed. New York and London: Plenum Press.

United Nations
  1976 *River basin development: Policies and planning*. 2 volumes. Proceedings of the United Nations Interregional Seminar on River Basin and Interbasin Development in Budapest, Hungary, 1975. New York: United Nations.

Waterbury, John
  1972 *The Cairo workshop on land reclamation and resettlement in the Arab world*. American Universities Field Staff Reports Service, Northeast Africa Series, vol. 18, issue 1.
  1977 *The Nile stops at Aswan. Part I: The Development of the Nile River system*. American Universities Field Staff Reports Service, Northeast Africa Series, vol. 22, issue 1.
  1979 *Hydropolitics of the Nile Valley*. Syracuse: Syracuse University Press.

Watson, James L.
  1974 Restaurants and remittances: Chinese emigrant workers in London. In *Anthropologists in cities*, ed. George M. Foster and Robert V. Kemper. Waltham, Mass.: Little, Brown and Co.

1975   *Emigration and the Chinese lineage:* The Mans in Hong Kong and *London.* Berkeley: University of California Press.

Weil, Simone
1952   *The Need for roots.* New York: G. P. Putnam.

Westermeyer, Joseph
1978   Ecological sensitivity and resistance of cultures in Asia. *Behavior Science Research* 13:109–23.

Wilson, Monica
1971   *Religion and the transformation of society: A Study in social change in Africa.* New York: Cambridge University Press.

Wisely, William H.
1972   People, ecology, and the Aswan High Dam. *Civil Engineering* 42(2): 37–39.

World Bank
1978   *Agricultural land settlement: A World Bank issues paper.* Washington, D.C.: World Bank.
1979   *Memorandum on social issues associated with involuntary resettlement in bank financial projects.* Washington, D.C.: World Bank.

Young, William
1978   Politics and social order in a Nubian novel. Photocopy.

Index

Absenteeism, male. *See* Labor migration

Abu Simbel: economic advantages at, 121, 122, 142; preservation of, 33; resettlement at, 122-23, 124

Agricultural issues in resettlement, 84-85, 162-63

Agriculture: in lake region, 120, 122-23; in New Nubia, 75-82, 84-85; in Old Nubia, 12, 13-14, 25, 77-78. *See also* Food and water supply

Animal husbandry: in New Nubia, 74, 103; in Old Nubia, 12-13

Anthropology of resettlement, 154-55, 156, 178-79, 180-183

Antiquities, preservation of, 33-34

Associations (clubs), Nubian: function of, 22, 82, 94, 101-2, 133, 135-36, 139, 149; and relocation in lake region, 121-22, 123-24, 127-28, 136, 141-42

Aswan High Dam: controversy over, 27-28; environmental and political aspects of, 4, 28-30, 34; Nubians' attitude toward, 31-32. *See also* Water resources and land development

Ceremonies and customs: changed in resettlement, 65-66; in Old Nubia, 17, 18, 19, 20-21

Children: and educational issues, 79, 93, 148, 167; and family life abroad, 143, 145-46; and resettlement schemes, 166-67

Communality. *See* House design, cultural importance of; Identity/Communality; Openness/Closedness; Village characteristics, cultural importance of

Community services: in New Nubia, 88-89, 90-91, 92, 93, 94-96; in Old Nubia, 17, 90, 92, 93

Cooperatives: agricultural, 76-77, 123; fishing, 130; multipurpose, 122-24

Coping strategies: and house design, 57, 63-64, 68; and labor migration, 12, 31-32, 112-13, 140, 147, 149; resettlement, 50-51, 53-54, 65, 97, 100-101, 103-6, 110-111, 119-20, 128-29, 163-64, 170, 180-181

Crops. *See* Agriculture

Demography: and labor migration, 13, 82-84, 98-99, 130, 132, 137-40; in lake region, 130-131; of New Nubia, 57, 83, 94-95, 98; of Old Nubia, 9-10, 11, 12, 13, 17, 98

Dependency syndrome, 85, 110, 162-63, 165-66

Development policies for resettlement, 79, 84-85, 89, 122-23, 129, 130-132, 153-57, 160, 163-64, 165-66, 168

Disease and health problems, 59, 67-69, 73, 89-90, 94-95, 111, 116-17, 118

193